NEITHER YOUR HONEY
NOR YOUR STING

NEITHER YOUR HONEY
NOR YOUR STING

BERNARD KOPS

Robson Books Ltd

Acknowledgement is made to Carta, Jerusalem, for permission to use certain drawings, reprinted from "The Four Seasons of Israel".

Design: Sylvia Wiener
Artwork: Skater & Co.

First published simultaneously in cased and paperback editions in Great Britain in 1985 by Robson Books Ltd., Bolsover House, 5-6 Clipstone Street, London W1P 7EB. Text copyright © 1985 Bernard Kops, drawings copyright © 1985 Martin Wiener

British Library Cataloguing in Publication Data

Kops, Bernard
    Neither your honey nor your sting.
    1. Israel—History
    I. Title
    956.94   DS117

    ISBN 0-86051-355-6
    ISBN 0-86051-355-1 Pbk

Printed in Great Britain by St Edmundsbury Press Ltd, Bury St Edmunds, Suffolk

For Erica, from Bernard

For my Father and Mother, Harry and Anna,
from Martin

Why can't the Jews live a quiet life? From the time they were born the Jewish people have never been out of the news. They are the great survivors of history. Why? They take nothing for granted. Just look at their humour. Joking is survival, balancing on a tightrope. Jewish mothers soothing their children might reassure: "One door closes, another door opens." But the Jewish humorist, more of a realist, puts it another way: "One door closes, another door closes." "Someone was nice to you? Careful, you'll suffer for it later." "You live and learn... well, you live."

Jews seem to survive impossible situations, laughing sometimes, crying sometimes. Their story is like a river; it twists and turns, it snakes through time, it loops and rises and falls back on itself, sometimes a dribble, sometimes a torrent. It surges past despots and dreamers, poets and fools, cowards and queens, heroes and tyrants. It is an umbiblical cord. The past is ever-present.

So do the Children of Israel live happily ever after? That'll be the day!

Balaam wants to curse the
people of Israel. "That's
not on," God thunders.
"In that case,"says Balaam,
"I shall bless them." God
remains adamant: "Give
them neither your honey
nor your sting."
(Numbers Rabah XX 10)

In this book I try to tell the
story of the Jews as it is,
neither cursing nor
blessing...

Abraham Born in Ur, 2000 BCE.

Jewish history begins with this great father of the Jewish people. Like most Jews he is restless and wants to be somewhere else. One day he takes off with his entire family, leaves his native city and searches for a new land.

He crosses the river Euphrates and this is why he and his people are called Hebrews—"Ivrim", those who came from the other side. Abraham somehow acquires a most amazing concept. He believes in the one god. Up until now gods and people are easily destroyed; you enter a temple, smash an idol to the ground and presto! the god is shattered and his followers scattered into oblivion. Abraham's concept is an act of sheer intellectual genius. If you have one invisible god, he cannot be destroyed.

Abraham's god is the god within you;

     he is everywhere, anywhere.

          He is the voice of your own conscience;

              he is the ultimate truth to be sought for;

                  he is eternal.

Thus the faith of Abraham and his people cannot be shattered; it will survive all other people and this people will survive all other people. Abraham loves his god (the feeling is mutual). For this act of unique recognition God gives Abraham something special in return—the promise of the land of Canaan, a homeland for Abraham and all his descendants. Abraham journeys through many lands with his wife, Sarah, and his children and his servants and his cattle and the cooking oil and his sons-in-law; and he takes his one indestructable god with him, seeking his promised land.

Abraham eventually finds the Promised Land; the fertile pastures near Hebron, under the terebinth trees upon the hills of Canaan.

Jacob is Abraham's grandson. Not altogether a nice guy. By subterfuge he manages to extract a blessing from his father, Isaac, a blessing the old patriarch had intended for his twin brother, Esau. But he is remembered for something far more important. One day, after crossing a river, Jacob bumps into a stranger. They decide to have a wrestling match. He wins and the stranger now reveals his true identity. He is an angel, a messenger of God. He gives Jacob a new name, "Israel, He who struggled with God." It sounds right, it fits. From now on the children of Jacob are known as the Children of Israel.

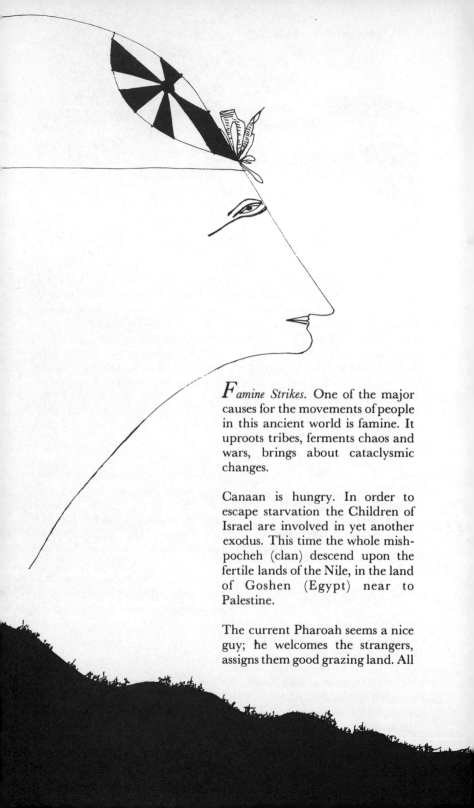

*F*amine Strikes. One of the major causes for the movements of people in this ancient world is famine. It uproots tribes, ferments chaos and wars, brings about cataclysmic changes.

Canaan is hungry. In order to escape starvation the Children of Israel are involved in yet another exodus. This time the whole mishpocheh (clan) descend upon the fertile lands of the Nile, in the land of Goshen (Egypt) near to Palestine.

The current Pharoah seems a nice guy; he welcomes the strangers, assigns them good grazing land. All

is well. The Children of Israel live here for many years, in peace. Time passes; the good Pharoah hits the dust.

Rameses II This Pharoah is a different kettle of fish. He is a man with big ideas, illusions of grandeur, the man who would be god. He wants a place in history and certainly gets it. He causes the word "Pharoah" to stink throughout history. He is clever, expansive and, like most tyrants, gets carried away with his own power.

*E*xodus. Moses gets God to afflict the Egyptians with terrible punishments. At first Pharoah refuses to listen to reason, but eventually he has no choice. **"Okay Moses, on your way!"** The

Children of Israel are on the move again, through opening oceans, across scorching deserts, starving, desperate, following their stern leader, who suddenly decides to go mountain climbing.

No sooner is his back turned than the Children of Israel behave like naughty children again, forgetting their one god, worshipping a golden calf. When Moses comes down from Mount Sinai he is furious with them, but his authority is restored and he reveals the Ten Commandments, the new rules that he has brought down from Sinai, rules that are going to change the world.

Every year until this present day, Jews celebrate this occasion; they dance in the street, hugging the Torah, the five books of Moses brought down from the mountain so many centuries ago.

These rules make good sense, commonsense. They are moral, ethical. The concept is brilliant; it marks the first great leap forward for mankind.

Moses is the great patriarch of Jewish history; he is exceptional. Apart from everything else he can achieve something no other human can achieve—he can get all the Jews to move in the same direction. This is genius indeed.

Moses had the vision, the dream to lead all his people to the Promised Land. The myth becomes substance, but not for Moses. He dies on Mount Nebo, above the Mountains of Judah. But the Promised Land does become a reality. It is Joshua who leads the Children of Israel down from the mountains and into the fertile valleys; the twelve tribes of Israel settle in Canaan, the Promised Land.

And so the Children of Israel live happily ever after. That'll be the day!

And from that day to this the Jews have never been out of the news. Why? Why is the idea of the Promised Land so potent? Why has the dream persisted? Why can't the Jews live a quiet life?

Questions! Questions!

Why do the Jews ask so many questions, pose so many questions? Is this the reason Jacob's angel names them "Those who struggle with God"?

Biblical Cord. Jewish history flows on and on. It is a beautiful, incredible story; funny and tragic, impossible. But Jewish history is not a straight line. It is a river that twists and turns. It snakes through time. It loops, it rises, it falls, it turns back on itself; it finds its way against all the odds. Sometimes it is a torrent, sometimes a dribble, but it never loses its identity, from the source of time until this present day. It is relentless, it surges onward, past the battles, the triumphs, the defeats, the despair, the rejoicing. Past despots and dreamers, poets and fools, cowards and queens, heroes and tyrants.

And like the river the Jewish people survive, somehow; and history is written by the survivors. And the river sings, exploits, names. Names that light up civilisation, names that will last as long as the world.

Deborah 1150 BCE. Judge, prophet. She arouses Israelites against superior Canaanite forces. Beneath Mount Tabor she scores a great victory. Her song commemorating that victory survives, one of the oldest manuscripts preserved in the Hebrew language.

Samson Tough guy. Falls for the wrong woman. Has a haircut; short back and sides. Doesn't like it; he brings down the barber shop.

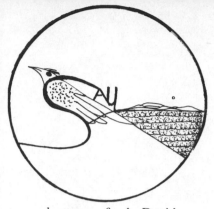

Saul 11th Century BCE. Farmer from the tribe of Benjamin; becomes the first king of Israel. Shy, courageous.

David 1000-960 BCE. Shepherd. Plays his harp and soothes the troubled King Saul. David is soon known as the "sweet singer of Israel." He becomes a warrior and kills Goliath, the dangerous freak. David proves that a small man can bring down a giant. But he is all too human. Later, when king, he quashes a rebellion fomented by his son, Absalom, who is killed in the process. David is bereft. His words still clutch at the heart.

"Oh my son Absalom... would I had died for thee..."

David is largely remembered for immortal psalms. Until now the Children of Israel are said to worship a jealous, wrathful god, a thundering father. But David changes all this: he sings another side of god—a gentle god, a god of love, a god who protects, a shepherd, a god of salvation. David's psalm sings...

"... Yea, though I walk through the valley of the shadow of death I shall fear no evil... for thou art with me..."

Solomon 961-920 BCE: Son of David and Bathsheba. Is said to have a thousand wives and mistresses. What is he trying to prove? Nevertheless he is said to be wise and stinking rich. His fabulous love song has been top of the pops for a few thousand years. He sings

"Come, let me kiss thee with kisses on thy mouth..."

Hot stuff. Oh yes, he also builds the great temple in Jerusalem.

After the death of Solomon, the Israelite nation starts to disintegrate, splits into two. Israel, the larger nation is in the north. The smaller kingdom is called Judah: it has little influence but its capital is Jerusalem. Much of the early Bible is written now.

In the middle of the eighth century BCE, Sargon, King of Assyria, invades Israel, destroys her army. The Ten Tribes are dispersed and the Children of Israel are deported to the far reaches of the Assyrian kingdom. The smaller nation, Judah, survives for the time being.

Isaiah 740-701 BCE. During these days of despair a new prophet emerges. He has a vision, a world where mankind will live in love and peace. "Awake and sing, all ye who dwell in dust..." His words, engraved in marble opposite the United Nations building in New York, challenge us today. "They shall beat their swords into ploughshares, and their spears into pruning hooks; nation shall not lift up sword against nation, neither shall they learn war anymore."

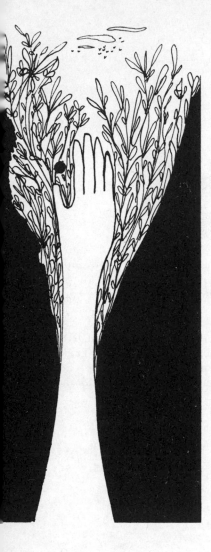

The Children of Israel are still in exile, but they never lose their longing for the land of Israel: in Jews it seems to go with breathing. One psalm sums it all up, it expresses the eternal longing of the Jews for their own homeland.

"By the rivers of Babylon,
  there we sat down,
Yea, we wept, when we remembered Zion.
Upon the willows we hanged
  our harps.
Those who captured us told
  us to sing,
"Sing us a song about
  Zion!"
How can we sing the Lord's
  song in a strange land?
If I forget thee oh Jerusalem
  let my right hand forget her
  cunning..."

6 13 BCE. Nineveh, the Assyrian capital, falls to the invading Persian and Babylonian armies. The Assyrian nation is defeated.

5 86 BCE. Nebuchadnezzar II, Babylonian king, invades Judah, captures Jerusalem. Solomon's temple is destroyed. Jewish leaders are deported to Babylon and used as slave labour; others are deported to Egypt, also forced into slavery. Wherever they are they never lose their dream of returning to their homeland.

5̲40 BCE. Cyrus the Great. This Persian king proves to be an enlightened monarch. He invades mighty Babylon and destroys the power of this tyrannical empire. Cyrus frees the enslaved Jews. They can now worship their own one god, celebrate their festivals, return to their own promised land. One way tickets to Jerusalem are in hot demand.

It is now 538 BCE. The Temple in Jerusalem is rebuilt. Bricklayers, plasterers and decorators are busy everywhere, giving a new shine to the old city that has fallen into decay. People smile again, go to parties.

Listen to this—can you believe it? There now follows a few hundred years of peace. The Jews are having a nice quiet spell, just quarrelling among themselves. **Did I say quiet spell**?

A̲lexander the Great 336-323 BCE. A new giant enters the stage of world history. This King of Macedonia destroys the might of the Persian Empire, conquers lands as far as India, dominates the whole of the Middle East. But Alexander is no tyrant; indeed he is supremely intelligent and tolerant. Jewish arts and crafts boom under his rule. Jewish trades flourish and there is cross-fertilisation between Jewish and Greek thought—a friendly argument concerning law and religion.

After Alexander's death the early books of the Bible are translated into Greek. Jewish ethics and ideas are no longer confined to a small area around Palestine. Suddenly the Jews have lift-off. They begin to receive international coverage, to influence other people.

1̲75-163 BCE. Another nasty hits the scene. He is Antiochus IV, King of Syria, soon to be known as Antiochus the Madman, overlord of the Land of Israel.

R̲ome becomes a world power; the Roman war machine grinds across the frontiers. Greece and Macedonia fall; Asia Minor and Syria are invaded. Nothing can stop the might of Rome.

A̲ntiochus tries to defend his kingdom and tries to Hellenize (make Greek) the Jews. He declares himself God, plunders and desecrates the Temple, attempts to get the Jews to worship his idols. The fool! He obviously hasn't read his history books. Who can get the Jews to give up their god? Scores are tortured, put to death. The smell of rebellion is in the air.

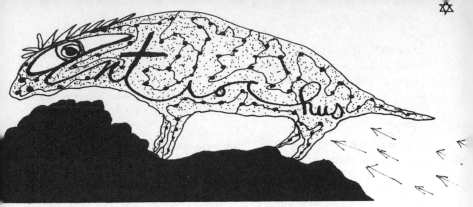

The Maccabees 168 BCE. Mattathias, a priest from the village of Modi'in, and his five sons, rise up against Antiochus. Guerrilla warfare spreads; the small revolt grows into open rebellion. The revolutionary movement is led by Judah, third son of Mattathias. Soon his fame spreads throughout the world, throughout time. He is known as Judah the Maccabee (The Hammer). In 164 BCE Jerusalem is liberated. The law of Moses is restored. This glorious moment lives in Jewish history. Hannukah, the Festival of Light, commemorates the famous victory of Judah the Maccabee and his courageous band of brothers.

Hillel 75 BCE-19, is a poor boy born in Babylonia. His parents must be proud; he does so well and becomes a great scholar. He is the author of the famous quote

"Do not unto others that which you would not have them do unto you."

Years later Jesus slightly rearranges this golden rule, so that it becomes "Love thy neighbour as thyself." Hillel has the concept: Jesus captures the headlines.

Herod 37 BCE. A Jewish boy, but not so nice. He becomes king, but he is a puppet of Rome. Intelligent, efficient and cunning, he is not entirely bad. He loves parties and going to shows, and there is peace for thirty years under his rule. But, like a mafia boss, he has dirty fingers in many pies. He has his wife, his three sons and his mother-in-law put to death. Would you want him for an uncle? His rule marks the end of Jewish independence.

Salome is Herod's granddaughter. The first stripper in history. She dances the dance of the seven veils and demands the death of John the Baptist. Maybe she just wants to get ahead.

Roman rules, not OK. A busy, desperate time. Chaos is king; events jam together in wild confusion; everything seems to be falling apart.

Jesus Born Joshua. Like all Jewish boys he is circumcised and at the age of thirteen can read the law (although the barmitzvah ceremony was only invented in the 15th century, so Jesus's parents don't have a catering problem). He becomes a member of the Essene sect, a strict male group concerned with ritual purity. He soon thinks of himself as a prophet who has the answer for everyone. Prophets proliferate at this time, but he convinces some others of his divine mission. To most Jews, however, he is a nice Jewish boy who mixes with the wrong company. He always sees himself as a Jew; indeed the Last Supper is a Passover meal. Others see him as Messiah and break away from Judaism. But he says "I come not to change the law, but to impose it."

Herod dies but the illusion of independence that he tried to convey does not survive his death.

We are now in the 1st-2nd Century. Behold the taxman cometh and stingeth everyone without mercy. Violence grows; the streets are unsafe.

30 About now Jesus Christ calls himself King of the Jews. He is put to death by the Romans.

Florus, 66, Roman Procurator This latest overlord combines cruelty, greed and stupidity: it proves to be a lethal mixture. He orders the desecration of the Temple. Serious riots occur; Florus retaliates and hundreds of citizens of Jerusalem are murdered. Rebellion blazes and spreads like fire. All Judea and Galilee are in open revolt; the Roman garrison in Jerusalem is destroyed and the Roman army is sent to Syria to restore order. The Jewish army traps them in a gorge at Beth Horon; six thousand Roman soldiers are killed. It is a humiliating defeat for Rome.

Titus takes command. The wrath of Rome descends and Jericho is smashed.

70 Jerusalem is besieged, the Temple destroyed. Only the Western Wall remains among the ruins. Resistance collapses; Jerusalem falls.

But the Jews do not become a subject race. The Torah, the holy books are not destroyed. The Pharisees preserve the teaching and the traditions; the Jewish religion and the people are thus guaranteed continuity. But the tragedy cannot be underestimated: the Land of Israel is lost to the Children of Israel.

These are desperate days... Thousands flee the land, scatter in all directions, but individual actions, certain names illuminate the dark.

Masada 73. This Zealot fortress is under the command of Eleazar who has already annihilated a Roman garrison. A thousand Jewish troops and their families withstand a prolonged Roman siege. The fortress, high on a rock above the desert, defies the iron fist of Rome. In the end the power of Rome prevails. But even then the Jews refuse to surrender, preferring mass suicide to relinquishing their faith, their own one god. When the Romans finally break through the defences only two women remain alive. Masada is a desperate hand of light in the dark landscape of defeat.

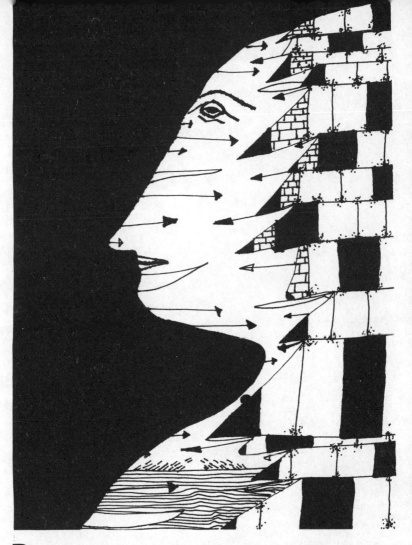

Bar Kochba (Son of the Star) 132-135, this brilliant young man decides to defy the Romans: he leads a Jewish army against the army of occupation. There is victory after victory until the bully is on the run. Town after town is liberated. People believe in miracles again; they dance in the street and when Jerusalem is recaptured everyone goes mad. Bar Kochba is declared head of the state; some even call him Messiah.

For two years Judea enjoys complete independence. But it is not to be. The dream of freedom remains only a dream. Hadrian gathers his legions and Bar Kochba is defeated. He and his men die defending Betar. Rome regains control; the iron fist falls again with terrible vengeance.

R*ome Rules*. The dark descends.

Another exodus is under way.

The   great dispersal begins and the Jews a r e s c a t

The loss of the Land of Israel has catas

Micah, a great Hebrew pr

" a light unto

over many continents.

consequences for the Jewish people.

tated that the Jewish people are to be ...

ons".

is almost extinguished— but not quite.

reat power, a dream, a hope of returning

now pervades the lives of every Jew forced to leave the Holy Land.

The loss of the Land of Zion paradoxically

gives immediate birth to the dream of regaining that

lost land. The dream that is the

root of Zionism.

Diaspora. A Greek word meaning "scattering".

This is a scattering with a vengeance. No other people have been scattered quite like the Jews. They seem to have this predilection for extremes; escaping from persecution they scatter in all directions, seeking peace in far lands.

But the cord with the Holy Land is never completely severed. Some Jews remain, in the heart of darkness, guardians of the golden city of Jerusalem.

And in Galilee, around 200, Rabbi Yehudah Ha-Nasi compiles and edits the Mishna, the body of Jewish law.

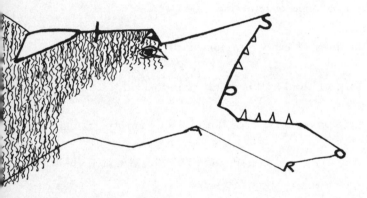

However, the mass exodus is inexorable. The Jews are on the move again, their most valuable possessions—their god, religion, law, ethics, skills, recipes, cooking pots, sense of humour. They even take their language with them, using it for prayer.

They settle all over the Roman world, and further. Italy, Greece, Spain, France, Asia Minor, the Arabian Peninisula, you name it. Babylon is also now an important centre of Jewish life.

Abba Arikha 219, known as Rav, an outstanding rabbi in Israel, returns to Babylon and expands the Mishna until it becomes the Talmud. This momentous work covers all aspects of Jewish life and faith and has a far-reaching effect in the world.

The Jews travel far and wide. They have not yet reached Britain; Jews like a suntan and no doubt have heard about the British weather. But they have reached India. As early as 175 BCE Jews have been arriving in India. They have now established a thriving community in Bombay. Called Bene Israel, they are split into two sections: black Jews and white Jews. The two groups refuse to mix with each other, which proves that Jews can be just as stupid as everyone else.

The Jews reach China. It is obvious, therefore, that Marco Polo gets it all wrong; he thinks noodles are a Chinese invention. Little does he know, otherwise he would have written a book, Spaghetti and the Jewish Problem.

Wherever they settle, the Jews do well and they develop in diverse ways, earning their living as artisans, craftsmen, street traders and farmers, and they dominate the rag trade. Soon they open kosher restaurants, but others please their parents even more by becoming doctors, lawyers, accountants. Although they take root in far-flung lands they are never swallowed by the indigenous people. One invisible thread holds them all together, binds them as a people. "Perhaps tomorrow Jerusalem." This prayer, this one incantation, protects them from all encroaching cultures.

Back in the Holy Land, Diocletian,
the Roman Emperor,
is managing to restore order.
Synagogues are shooting up all
over Galilee; the Jews who remain in
the Land of Israel are also doing well.

"In the Holy land there is a large town with a considerable population consisting only of Jews. This town is called in Aramaic, Lod." (Eusebius, Ecclesiastical historian, 384-420).

Rome. Around this time the iron fist holds an olive branch—at least as far as the Jews are concerned. Freedom of worship and the practice of Jewish law are guaranteed. Jews don't have to belong to the armed forces. This must be good for the Jews; to belong is nice, but to columns of Roman legions? What sort of trade is that for a nice, restless, individualistic Jewish boy? It's hardly a living. More like a dying. This is the good news.

So what's the bad news? Wait! Not everything in the world is coming up roses; racial intolerance is once again raising its obscene head.

Isfahan Persia. Jews become second-class citizens. The walls of their houses cannot be built as high as those of the Muslims who live next door. Neither are Jews allowed to ride horses in the street. In the bathroom maybe?

The year is 300 and the latest census suggests there are three million Jews alive and kicking at this time. Some convert to Christianity, but the main body remains faithful to the faith.

425 The Goths capture Rome. But the Roman way of life captures the Goths, who convert to Christianity. Under Gothic rule the power of the Roman Catholic church spreads to many lands. Missionaries go out with burning zeal and cold convictions. Jews are considered to be a danger to the religious unity of the Empire and harsh laws are passed against them. The real Dark Ages begin.

460 In Isfahan things are going from bad to worse; all Jewish children are converted by force.

By 500 the Jews are firmly established in Avignon, Marseilles, Ravenna, Genoa, Venice, Rome. They begin to migrate north across the Alps into Germany.

Meanwhile: "Nazareth!

So great is the beauty of the Jewish women of the town that you will not find more beautiful women among the Jews in the length and breadth of this land." (Antonius the Martyr, Christian pilgrim in Palestine, towards end of 6th Century).

Mohammed—Prophet of Islam 570-632 His new creed bursts upon the world and spreads like wildfire. He shares many Jewish prophets. At first he is convinced there is no essential difference between Judaism and his new faith, indeed, he hopes to win the Jews to embrace his faith, even

adapting some rituals to accommodate the Jews. One of his wives, Sarah, is of Jewish origin. So far so good. But his hopes are not fulfilled; the Jews do not seem to need a new intermediary with God. They remain unconvinced and spurn this new prophet. But the birth of Islam is to have an overwhelming effect upon the destiny of the Jewish people. Mohammed never forgives the Jews for rejecting him and he becomes hostile towards the Jews of Medina. The Jews in the rest of Arabia continue to enjoy a good relationship with their Muslim neighbours.

Sisebut 616. This fanatical Visigoth becomes the King of Spain. The terror gathers momentum.

Christians are not allowed to consult Jewish doctors. Jews cannot hold public office. Psalms must not be sung at funerals. The dead must be buried in silence. Intermarriage is forbidden.

Jewish children are torn from their parents and forcibly converted. Many Jews are faced with a choice, "death or conversion?" Some choose the latter and are baptised. They become Christians, but practise their religion in secret. In their hearts they remain Jews. These are known as Marranos (swine).

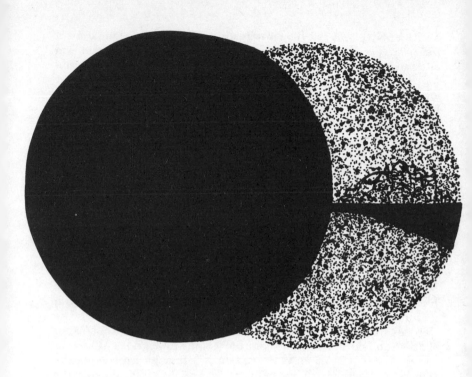

Heraclitus was Emperor of Byzantium 610-641. Fearing the rising power of Islam, he forbids all religions except Christianity. The Kings of Burgundy and Lombardy follow his example. Bigotry becomes rampant in the Christian world. Ignorance and intolerance become respectable. Racial hatred takes root, poisons the atmosphere. A pattern is established that will have terrible consequences in the future. The twisting paths starting from bigotry will end in a straight, wide road leading to the gas chambers.

Charlemagne, 768-814, a Frankish king, becomes Roman Emperor. He is enlightened and protects the Jews of his vast empire. They are given security of life and property and are free to be the sort of Jews they want to be. When he dies, his son, Louis the Pious, succeeds him. The bishops have a jolly good try to influence the new ruler against his Jewish subjects, but they fail. Louis continues the benign policies of his father.

Khazar Kingdom 700-1083. Interesting sidelight to the long story of the Jews. The Khazars are a Turkish or Finnish nomadic tribe who settle in the lower Volga regions of Russia. They become a powerful state and extend westwards as far as Kiev. 40,000 Khazar soldiers fight for the Byzantine Emperor in his war against Persia. One day King Bulan and four thousand of his nobles decide they want to become Jews. They convert to Judaism and make contact with Jews in other lands. This conversion receives wide coverage. Judah Ha-Levi, the great Jewish poet of Spain, believes them to be one of the lost tribes of Israel. The Khazars remain tolerant towards all other religions and they maintain power for over three hundred years. Eventually the Russian Archduke Yaroslav destroys them on the banks of the Volga. The year is 1083. They disintegrate. Who knows? If they had survived there might well be now a Khazar consulate in Golders Green or the Bronx.

700 For centuries now in Europe and Byzantium, Jews are being cowed by oppression and persecution for the so-called "murder" of Jesus. The Babylonian centre of Judaism is in decline, but the Jewish communities of North Africa and Spain are on the ascent. The Vandals are on the move; the Barbarians have driven the Romans out of Spain and north Italy. The might of Rome disintegrates. Wherever you find Barbarians and Vandals, you will find Jewish contingents alongside—fighting, helping, rejoicing at the defeat inflicted upon the Christians and the Byzantines.

The Golden Age

711 Tarik, the Moorish General, crosses from Morocco, enters Spain with his army. Within four years all Spain is under Arab domination. The Arabs show moderation and tolerance towards Jews, who welcome them with open arms.

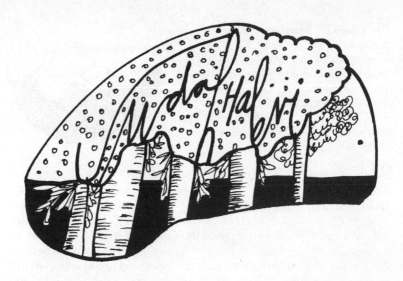

Under Arab rule Spain becomes a land of learning, science, poetry and music. Reason reigns, in strict contrast to the turbulent desperation of the rest of Europe. Beautiful synagogues are built, magnificent gardens are laid out. In Granada, Toledo and Cordoba Jewish communities flourish. Jews adopt Arab names, learn Arabic and easily adapt to the Arab way of life without relinquishing one iota of faith. The Arabs are quick to recognise Jewish intellect and culture and soon Jews are appointed to high positions in the fast-growing administration. Many Jews are employed directly by the Caliph, the ruler of Spain. This new stability creates a climate of hope, for life has now become more than mere survival. The atmosphere is absolutely right; creativity soon bursts out all over the place; everything in the garden is coming up orange trees. For more than five hundred years Jews are going to enjoy peace and security here in Spain; philosophers will argue again, thinkers will think and poets will sing.

Careful when you leave your house; you may trip over a poet or philosopher. They are everywhere. To name but a few:

Hasdai Ibn Shaprut (915-970)
Eminent physician and linguist.
Doctor, friend and advisor to the
Caliph. A leading member of the
Jewish community, he supports
Jewish learning, scholars, students,
poets, writers; becomes extremely
influential in the wide diplomatic
world.

Samuel Ibn Nagdela (993-1056). A grocer from Malaga,
specialising in spices. He has a phenomenal mind and speaks six
languages; he is also a philosopher, mathematician and Hebrew
scholar. People seek his advice about everything. His learning and
style of letter writing so impresses the Caliph's Grand Vizier that he
makes Sam his secretary. When the Vizier dies, the Caliph appoints
Sam in his place, so Sam moves into the palace in Granada and lives in
fantastic splendour, greatly enjoying his new position. The title
Samuel, the Prince in Israel, is conferred upon him and his fame
spreads far and wide. But Sam remains modest, no doubt still smelling
of spices.

Solomon Ibn Gabirol (1021-1058). Great poet whose celebrated
Keter Malkhut (Royal Crown) becomes part of the liturgy for the Day
of Atonement. Like all of these poets of Spain he dreams of Israel and
loves God.

"Before I was born, your love enveloped me, you turned
nothing into substance and created me...,"

he sang. He still sings. His work survives. All the poets of Spain sing to
us still; their work touches something deep within us, recognises the
dichotomy, loving where we are, longing for somewhere else.

Moses Ibn Ezra (1055-1139). No more, no less can be said for
Moshe.

Abraham Ibn Ezra (1092-1167). Or for Abe. Poet.

But the crowning glory of poets, of poetry was...

Judah **Ha-Levi** (1075-1141). Born in Toledo. He is a keen student of the Bible, also an eminent physician, scholar of Arabic literature, learned in the fields of astronomy, mathematics and philosophy. As he gets older he develops a passionate longing for the Land of Israel and writes his famous poems Songs of Zion.

In his old age he decides to pack up and "return" to the Holy Land. But the journey is long and dangerous. There are pirates on the seas and land journeys are nightmares owing to the warring tribes and thieves. But Judah cannot be dissuaded. He makes the long journey, visiting Jewish communities as he goes, each in turn trying to dissuade him from going any further. Legend says that when he reaches the Gates of Jerusalem he falls to his knees to kiss the holy ground and is killed by the horse of an angry Arab rider.

Others say he died in Egypt. Who knows? But there is no doubt about his poetry.

> "My love washes her clothes in the water
> Of my tears, and her brilliance makes them dry
> Having my two eyes, she does not need
> Well water. Her beauty contains the sun."

But in the Jewish world the impossible is always possible. Even the crowning glory can be crowned. You can always go one better, even than excellence. If you know of a great man, be assured there is always a greater man...

Moses **Ben Maimon (Maimonides)** (1135-1204). The peak of Jewish achievement in Spain is surely Maimonides. He is the most outstanding figure in the whole of this Golden Age. He practises medicine and his fame as a physician spreads. Rich, poor,

Jew, Spaniard, Moslem, they all come knocking on his door. The poor are treated free. He becomes an inspired teacher and interpreter of the law. He writes brilliant philosophical works, works that will have an effect upon other thinkers and philosophers, even in the distant future. One of his works is a code of Jewish law. It is called the Mishne Torah, the most important code of Jewish law since the completion of the Torah. This encyclopaedic work is written in a beautiful style. Another important work is Guide for the Perplexed. It clearly explains the principles and ideas of Judaism with philosophical and logical reasoning.

In his commentary on the Mishna we find his famous Thirteen Articles of Faith that declares the Jewish creed: "Ani ma'amin, be'emunah sh'leymah, b'viyat ha-mashiach/Ani ma'amin..."

"I believe in the coming of the Messiah, and even though he is late I still believe."

These words are set to music centuries later, in the darkest days of Jewish history, by a nameless victim in the Warsaw Ghetto. This song spreads to Jewish guerrilla units and to concentration camps. People sing these words as they walk into the gas chambers. The Golden Age is at an end. It has been almost a miracle set against the dark backdrop, the twisted bigotry of mediaeval Europe. But it has proved that persecution is not the only catalyst, not the only potent force that drives the Jewish people towards the dream of Jerusalem. Here in this Golden Age we have had poets and philosophers and our ordinary next-door neighbours living in peace and security, dreaming their dreams in harmonious surroundings. No hint of hatred; no fear of pogrom; yet still the same dream persists.

"Perhaps tomorrow Jerusalem."

Jews take nothing for granted; it's deep in the bones—to expect the unexpected. For if light follows dark, then dark can follow light. Spain was glorious. Unfortunately Spain is not the whole world; it is only part of the story.

The rest of Europe has other ideas.

The Hill of Darkness

These are the Middle Ages. The pagan people of Europe are slowly being converted to Christianity, but old beliefs die hard. Pagan superstition survives—belief in magic, witchcraft and wicked gods. The Jews are a convenient scapegoat. The Roman Catholic Church does nothing to discourage this hatred growing towards these strangers, these Jews who do not accept Christ.

From 1095 reports are reaching Europe of unholy happenings in the Holy Land. Christian pilgrims are mugged in Jerusalem by Seljuk

Turks. Some are imprisoned, even killed. Church leaders meet in Clermont, France. Pope Urban II summons kings, princes, knights, soldiers to form an army of Christians, to attack the Turks and Moslems in Palestine and recapture the Holy Places.

That meeting in Clermont becomes known by Jewish historians as the Hill of Darkness.

*T*he first Crusades take place and set off vicious attacks upon the Jews all over Europe. Jews are forced to accept baptism or massacre. Mobs run riot, seeking out Jews. 700 Jews are murdered in Worms. Entire communities are expelled and wander Europe seeking new homes. A plague, a disease, turns humans into beasts. No, sorry that's unfair to beasts; beasts rarely kill their own kind. The Jews draw together for security, for comfort, while the mobs rage outside. This festering disease will last four centuries.

Wherever they go on their journey to Jerusalem, under the flag of the cross, the Crusaders seek out Jews and kill them. By the time the Crusades end, a great wall of mistrust and fear separates Jew from Christian. Harsh laws are imposed upon the Jews. The Nazi codifiers of Nuremburg didn't have to look too far for inspiration. They took their old time religion and forced it in their own twisted way.

1 099 Jerusalem is captured by the Crusaders. Most of the Jews living there are murdered. Survival is now a day-to-day struggle, life a hand-to-mouth existence. All over the Diaspora there is no security and little hope. All aspirations are invested in the inviolable dream of Jerusalem. There is only one God and the promise of the Promised Land.

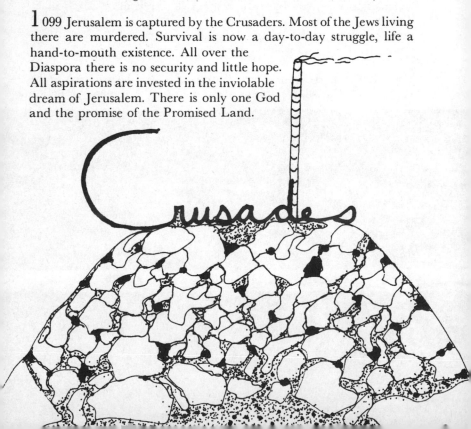

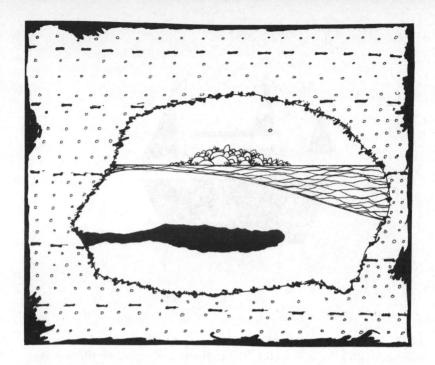

Jews huddle together in fear.

By 1187 the Crusaders have been defeated by Saladin. Jews again enjoy a measure of freedom in the Holy Land. The Jewish community in Jerusalem is increasing by leaps and bounds.

1144 Norwich. William, a young apprentice is found dead in a wood. There are no injuries on the body and obviously he has died of a fit, but the Jews are blamed. "They wanted William's blood for matzot for their Passover feast." The first "Jew hunts" begin.

1189 Richard I is crowned King of England. Attacks begin immediately upon the Jewish community in London. Many murdered.

1190 York. Jews are driven out of their living quarter, take refuge in the Castle "under the protection of the King". Some protection! They are besieged, but refuse to surrender. Mass suicide, like Masada, takes place. The men kill their own wives and children; then they kill each other.

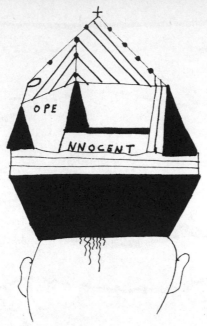

1211   Three hundred Rabbis from England and France grab their possessions and flee to the Holy Land. Some settle in Acre, the rest in Jerusalem.

1290   King Edward I orders all Jews to be expelled from England and Wales. They are given three months to pack up and get out.

Note: For England, read the rest of Europe. These scenes are happening everywhere. Pandora's box of hatred has been opened.

1306   France. The Jews have lived here for a thousand years; now they have just four weeks to get out. All property is confiscated. They go, they come back; they go, they come back. The old story.

1215   Yellow Badge edict. Pope Innocent III is far from innocent. He decrees that all Jews must wear a yellow badge to label them as outcasts; in some cases Jews must also wear pointed hats. This gives Holy Christian sanction for the tide of intolerance. Persecution gathers momentum; torturers and murderers are working overtime. The Yellow Badge becomes the distinguishing identity mark to be used by persecutors of the Jews in the future.

From 1348-49 The Black Death reigns. Plague sweeps through Europe. Millions die. Indeed half of the population of Europe is wiped out. So what caused the plague? Who are the perpetrators? You guessed it. The Jews are blamed. The cry goes out, "The Jews have poisoned the wells."

Jewish ritual laws of purity and cleanliness probably give the Jews some immunity from the dreaded disease. But these are the Middle Ages, do not expect reason. Expect only rampaging mobs and the plunging of knives. The plague on the face of Europe corresponds to the plague in the hearts of the people in Europe. You could say they deserve each other—except that one pities the ignorance and the grinding poverty of the masses of Europe, living their lives in desperation and fear while their princes feast, cocooned from the terror in the streets.

Nuremburg Germany 1298 Entire Jewish community butchered.

Poland 1265. King Boleslav grants Jews special protection: "Jewish Immigrants Welcome!"

Poland reaps much benefit from new arrivals who open up new commercial enterprises, creating new markets for their hosts. But the terror created by the Black Death spreads to Poland, where for a time Jews experience the usual persecution and killing. A century later King Casimir the Great ascends to power and continues the enlightened policy of Boleslav. Jews are permitted to live and work everywhere; they are allowed to have a Chief Rabbi. Old men argue in Yiddish in the streets and women barter for fish in Yiddish in the markets. Hundreds of yeshivot (Academies of Higher Rabbinic Studies) are springing up all over the place. The non-Jewish upper classes are enjoying their new international connections in trade and finance; connections that the Jews have brought with them. So everyone is happy; there seems to be enough peace to breathe freely again (for the moment!).

In Palestine, around 1350, the Mamluks have restored calm. Jewish settlements are once more allowed. Jews begin to move from villages in Galilee to the urban community of Safad. Moslem residents complain about the extensive amount of Jewish building that is taking place.

Meantime, Spain is under Christian control. There have been long wars and the Arabs have been defeated. The Pope of Rome wants to deal harshly with all non-Christians, but King Alfonso is wise, he ignores diatribes and continues a liberal policy with his subjects. Moslems, Moors, Berbers, Jews and Christians are allowed to live together in peace and security. The Pyrenees act like a barrier, keeping out the hatred that affects the rest of Europe.

Pedro the Cruel is King of Castile. He doesn't live up to his name as far as the Jews are concerned. He is most kind to the "people of the book", but is the very last king to treat the Jews in a benign fashion. When he is deposed the Jews of Spain are forced to wear the dreaded badge of shame—the Yellow Star.

By 1391 the Jews of Spain have been free for five hundred years. They have got used to the luxury of living in peace; they have not expected persecution; they are not prepared for the blow that falls. The glint in the eye has been replaced by a furtive look of fear. You can feel the frightened atmosphere in the streets as the Jews hurry across the square. The Jews in Spain have caught up with their folk in the rest of Europe. Unfortunately. They huddle indoors, waiting for the next edict, the next racial attack. They don't have to wait very long.

Newsflash: Severe anti-Jewish riots break out in Seville! Thousands of Jews killed!
Riots spread all over Spain!
Toledo—hundreds massacred!
Barcelona! Entire Jewish community exterminated, 1,000 Jews perish!

Conversion. Granada is the only major Jewish settlement to survive. Granada is a small kingdom, still ruled by Moslems. But this is the black year in the rest of Spain. The persecution is so horrendous many Jews break under the strain. For the second time many accept baptism, become their own dreaded enemies—Christians! It must have been hell for them—imagine the inner torment.

But the converts, Marranos, are still Jewish at heart; this gives them some comfort. Three thousand years of being Jewish cannot be erased by overnight conversion. The pretend Christians do well, excel. They regain the high positions they formerly held in Spanish society. They intermarry into the nobility, the gentry. They enter law, the army, the civil service, even the church.

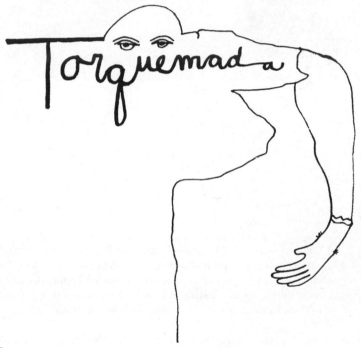

Thomas De Torquemada is born in Valladolid, Spain, 1420. A name that will turn spines into jelly when whispered in the future. In 1434 he becomes a priest. He is cold, austere, sincere and dedicated. He is a fanatical Christian who believes there is only one way, the way of Jesus Christ. All else is heresy and there is no room in this world for heresy. He soon rises up the Dominican hierarchy, believing that the Jews and the Moslems are undermining the religious and social life of Spain. These Dominicans become so fanatical in the pursuit of their faith, they become known as the Dogs of God.

*T*he Inquisition

In 1474 Isabella becomes Queen of Castille and marries Ferdinand of Aragon; thus most of Spain is joined together as one kingdom. Torquemada is the Queen's confessor and trusted advisor. A Catholic tribunal is established in Castille. Object? To carry out a purge; to smell out Marranos; to see if they truly believe in Jesus Christ.

Terror takes over. Torture is widespread, the torture chamber becoming the busiest place in Christendom. Traditional torturers are working overtime. But other methods of breaking people are used; more sophisticated techniques are being evolved. Modern brainwashing may well have learned many lessons from these dedicated inquisitors of Spain. You can be absolved and saved if you name names, if you recant in public, denounce others, friends and relatives also involved in the Jewish conspiracy. The Moscow trials, the Nazis, Senator McCarthy and his cronies, all these owe much to Torquemada and Co. The Inquisition draws its revenue from the heretics, from the goods and wealth of its victims.

The Spanish people suddenly lose their dignified humanity and join the witchhunt. Heresy becomes a national scourge to be eradicated at all costs. The methods work. The virus spreads until it affects the whole body of Spain. Dark, dark days.

1492 "In fourteen hundred and ninety two, Columbus sails the ocean blue." And his expeditions to the New World are financed by two Marrano merchants. There is a widespread theory that Columbus himself is also of Marrano extraction. Little wonder New York, New York is a wonderful town—it's Jewish.

But this year is notorious for a far more sinister event. A royal decree demands that all Jews be expelled from Spain within four months. A slow bell tolls. 200,000 Jews begin their journey into exile; out of the frying pan of Spain and into the fire of Europe. One long, great and wonderful chapter of Jewish life is over. Spain has inherited the sick, twisted madness that has infected the rest of the Christian world. The bell tolls for thee.

Ghetto (Probably from the Italian word "Borghetto", meaning borough or quarter). There has been an edict from Rome since 1180 that Jews are not allowed to live near Christians. This has largely been ignored. But in 1516 a further decree orders all Jews in Venice to move into one small quarter of the city; they are to be walled off from the rest of Venice. The doors are guarded day and night by Christian soldiers. No Jews allowed out after dusk, no Christians allowed in. On Sundays and holidays Jews are not allowed to leave the ghetto at all. Restrictions proliferate, indignity is piled on to insult. The Jews are to be an example for all those who refuse to accept the Christian church.

Ghettos are set up all over Europe (except in Holland, an oasis of tolerance). But the Jews, like so often in their history, turn this humiliation into a sort of positive advantage. They grow even closer together. Life in the ghettos takes on a new vigour. The study of Torah, the celebration of the Sabbath and holidays, become the centre of focus. The emphasis on family life, that pivotal factor of the Jewish people, becomes intensified. The ghetto is to have an effect throughout the centuries; long after the imprisoning walls have come tumbling down, Jews still tend to cluster together.

48

Martin **Luther** 1483-1546.. A German religious reformer and founder of Protestantism. His translation of the Bible into German is outstanding. At first he condemns the Catholic church for its treatment of the Jews; indeed, he thinks highly of the Jews, hopes they will now convert to his form of Christianity. He should know better. The Jews remain unmoved. Gradually his attitude changes until he becomes a rabid and virulent anti-semite, pleading for the persecution, the damnation, of the race that spurns him. His ideas are used to poison the well that one day will irrigate the nightmares of modern Nazi Germany.

Where now? Not just a geographic question, also a philosophical one. "Where are we going?" "What are we doing?" The children of Abraham and Jacob are still wrestling with the angel, will never stop asking questions. Jewish mothers soothing their children might reassure: "One door closes, another door opens." But the Jewish humorist, more of a realist, might put it another way: "One door closes, another door closes." The door of Spain has been slammed! Portugal follows Spain with witch-hunts, forcible conversions and the great expulsion. Many Portuguese Marranos are not lucky enough to escape: they are burned in public in ceremonies called "Auto da fe" (Acts of Faith).

By 1517 the Holy Land has changed hands again. The Ottoman Turks are now top dogs. They welcome the Jews. Four centres of Jewish life thrive here. Jerusalem, Safad, Tiberias, Hebron. This door has opened for the Jews of Spain. Ten thousand refugees settle in Safad, more than a thousand in Jerusalem. The Spanish Jews do well in the Ottoman Empire and all seem to make a good living. Four more synagogues are built in Jerusalem. The Jews of the sixteenth century also work the Holy Land, make it fertile. Pierre Belon, a French doctor and traveller in Galilee, writes in 1547: "Today Jews are living in these villages and they have built up again all the places around the lake, starting fishing industries, and have once again made the earth fruitful where once it was desolate."

The Jews of Spain have also crossed the Straits of Gibraltar, finding refuge in North Africa. They enter the great cities — Cairo, Alexandria, Fez, Algiers. They work hard, but don't think they all do well. There are many poor Jews here, all struggling for a living. They and their descendants will be humbled by poverty for centuries hereafter.

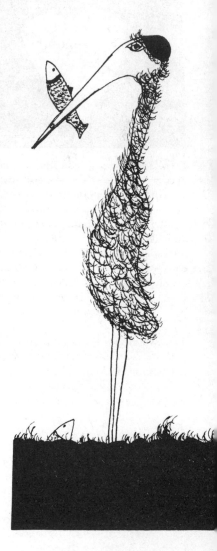

The Jews of Spain, now being scattered all over the world, are known as Sephardim, from the Hebrew word for Spain. To this day many speak Ladino, a mixture of Spanish and Hebrew. The Jews of Central and Eastern Europe are known as Askenazim, from the Hebrew for German, most of their forefathers having once resided in Germany.

The Jews find their feet in Constantinople which is just as well: they may need them again, quite soon, for moving on. Meanwhile they set up the first printing press in these parts. The Sultan is grateful, the atmosphere benevolent. So the Jews relax again, become doctors, lawyers, accountants and fishmongers.

France 1519-1559. Henry II, King of France, ardent Catholic, welcomes the Jews back into this land, guarantees them civil rights. Soon the King of Denmark will follow suit.

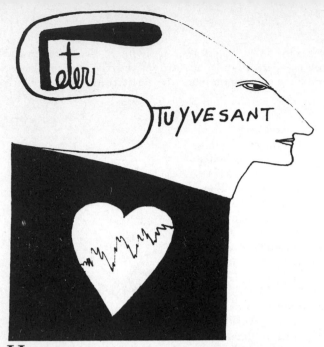

Holland. A new chapter begins, a relationship of mutual respect between the Dutch people and the Jews, a special relationship that will last and will benefit both peoples. Holland provides an enthusiastic haven for those Jews who are fleeing from the tyranny of Spain. Amsterdam, a thriving, open-minded city, especially welcomes the new arrivals and becomes the principal port of the low countries. Jewish financiers invest large sums in the Dutch West India Company. At the end of the sixteenth century Holland wins independence from Spain and immediately challenges the Spanish stranglehold on the oceans and, therefore, the trade with the East. Jewish bankers and merchants help to break this monopoly; the Dutch recognise their contribution.

1624 Portugal dominates large parts of Brazil. The Dutch decide to win this fabulous prize, and Jews provide funds and many young men to fight for Holland. The expedition is a success. Dutch Jews now flock to Dutch colonies. You can now find Jews in Cuba, Mexico and along the East Coast of what will become the United States of America.

1654 Marranos are seeking new homes in the New World. They land at New Amsterdam, a Dutch settlement. The Governor, Peter Stuyvesant, doesn't seem to like Jews; he is unwilling to accept them. Maybe he is not an anti-semite, maybe he just woke up with toothache this morning. But his employers, the Dutch West Indian Company are furious; their Jewish investors are putting on the screws, threatening that unless the Marranos are allowed into New Amsterdam they will divert all their wealth and expertise and offer the whole package to the French who have also settled along this coast. The pressure works and

Stuyvesant has to swallow his prejudice. The Jews enter New Amsterdam. The man mainly responsible for this pressure is a Marrano scholar. His name is Menasseh Ben Israel (1604-57). A close friend of the painter Rembrandt, he is one of the most powerful Jews in Amsterdam. Menasseh is brilliant, speaks nine languages, is a student of the Kabbalah and the Talmud. He has the notion that the Jews cannot be reassembled as one nation until they are readmitted into  Great Britain. He nobbles Oliver Cromwell, Lord Protector of England, Scotland and Ireland.

1655 Menasseh travels to England to try to convince the Puritans, who regard themselves as one of the lost tribes of Israel. He doesn't succeed at this point; there is great political opposition from the business community, but he does blaze a trail. Cromwell's tolerant attitude and Menasseh's pilgrimage finally pay off.

Marranos who have been living in England for some time now are granted the right to worship as they please in 1656. Thus the Jews are re-established in Great Britain; soon they will be joined by waves of immigrants, and Jewish communities will be established all over the land.

Spinoza 1632-77. Who would believe that a modest telescope lens grinder would become a major influence on Western philosophy? Baruch is a student of Torah and Talmud and his ideas are not unlike Maimonides'. At twenty-four years of age, the rabbis of Amsterdam have high hopes for this brilliant young man. Spinoza also has a great knowledge of ancient Greece and Rome. But soon he rejects many of Maimonides' principles and disagrees with orthodox Jewish thinking. The orthodox view is that "law derives from authority and authority ceases when its ability to enforce obedience ceases." Baruch believes that every man has the right to think for himself. He also questions the divine origin of the Bible. This upsets the Christians. The Jews are afraid that if they support Baruch the Christians will turn against them. They offer Baruch a life pension if he refrains from publishing. Baruch says publish and be damned. And that's precisely what happens. In 1656 he is excommunicated by the rabbis of Amsterdam. He is cut off by the Jewish community and even estranged from his own family. Thus this great man is tragically lost to his people and dies alone at the age of forty-five. Apart from his incredible contribution to Western thought he is also remembered for his burning conviction that "... only after the Jewish people learn again to speak their ancient language and return to their homeland would God restore love to them." His ideas surely influence Herzl over two hundred years later. It comes down to this; "**Do it for yourself, don't leave it to God**." Or "**If you will it, it is no fairytale**." Survival is in your own hands. Don't wait for God, get on with it.

Europe has emerged from the dark. Things have been quite quiet for the Jews. BUT don't count your chickens! Jews never take anything for granted. It is reflected in their humour; it reminds us that the surface of civilisation is extremely thin. Jewish humour goes back a long way. It was born with Abraham; it's as old as the biblical cord. It comes out of struggle, suffering and hope, a strange amalgam of these elements. Joking is survival, balancing on the tightrope.

"Someone was nice to you? Careful, you'll suffer for it later."

"You live and learn . . . well, you live."

"Once bitten—twice bitten."

It is soft, human cynicism. Therefore the Jews are hardly surprised when a new tragedy occurs.

Poland 1648-56. The Polish lords are Roman Catholic. The peasants belong to the Russian Orthodox church. There is no love lost between the two groups. The Ukrainian peasants live under impossible conditions and hate their Polish landlord masters. The Jews have lived here in peace and security for hundreds of years. All this is about to be swept away. The only contact that most serfs have with their masters is through their agents who collect the taxes and manage their estates.

During the quiet years the Jews have been used by the Polish Upper Crust and have become their agents. The anger of the peasants spills over; the Jews are caught in the middle. The atavistic hatred of the simple mind soon floods to the surface again. The peasants rising against their masters take their revenge upon their representatives. "The Jews, kill the Jews!" The evil of racism is rampant once more.

Cossacks In Jewish minds this word does not conjure an image of brave, happy horsemen. No comrades singing nostalgic songs around the fire; no balalaikas strum. All that the Jews can hear are thundering hooves of death. Their name conjures fear in Jewish homes as they rampage across the large mass of Poland, led by Bogdan Chmielnicki, their leader. They are in revolt and they are revolting. And the Jews are left to their fate. The violence continues for eight years. When the cost is counted one hundred thousand Jews have been murdered and thousands have fled to the Balkans, Germany, Holland. The Chmielnicki massacres are seared into the Jewish ethos; he is the godfather of the modern pogroms.

The Promised Land seems an unredeemed fantasy. Jews are longing for deliverance, but the Messiah seems a long time coming. Yet the pupil is still ready. Surely now the master will appear? All Jewish life, all hope and expectations, are now focused on the Messiah; whole Jewish communities expect him. Messiah mania breaks out, takes over. "Any day now he will walk through that door and lead us to the Holy Land."

The Kabbalists (mystics who seek hidden truths in numbers and dates) are calculating the odds. They come up with a date. "The Messiah will arrive in . . .

Shabbtai Zevi, 1648, from Smyrna in Turkey. A handsome young man, born of Spanish refugees. Twenty-two years old, he stands up in synagogue and declares himself the Messiah. He picks the right year, the year predicted by the Kabbalists. As a child Shabbtai is manic-preparing himself for this great day. Is he a fool, is he a crook? No, he is Supermessiah! That's what a few people think, but the majority of the congregation are stunned. Probably he is sincere, with illusions of grandeur. But nothing exceeds like excess and his burning zeal is extreme. He wins over many disciples and they follow him to Jerusalem. Rabbis and scholars fall under his spell. Prayer books

are printed in Amsterdam, recognising his divinity. Jews all over the world are in a state of excitement, expectation. Many are winding up their businesses; dry cleaners are closing down. You can't contact your accountant, he's away from the office; she doesn't know when he'll be back. Everybody knows somebody who is preparing to pack their bags and follow their Messiah to the Holy Land. There is a feeling like the end of the world, like a giant volcano about to burst.

It does.

1666 Shabbtai goes to Constantinople to "depose the Sultan." But the Sultan makes the first move, arrests this "Messiah", confines him to a fortress in Gallipoli. Yet even now Shabbtai hangs on to his chutzpah. The Jewish masses of Turkey still heap him with honours; he holds court in the fortress, continuing to receive thousands of his followers. The Turkish authorities are furious and the Sultan plays his last trump. It works. Under threat of death Shabbtai is forced to convert to Islam. His followers are stunned. They cannot believe it at first, but then the truth dawns. They melt away and lick their wounds and the whole Messiah euphoria fizzles out. The Messiah has not yet come. He is expected, but will come in his own time. Darkness descends, hope flies out of the window. (You can get straight through to your accountant again.)

The story of the Jews is always bitter-sweet, always tragic and funny. But for now sweetness and comedy are taking a nap and the Jews are vulnerable again, and depressed—and still waiting.

In Palestine—Kfar Yasif. Agricultural village, perhaps the earliest sort of kibbutz, is established in Galilee, first half of the eighteenth century.

58

Poverty . Meanwhile, back in Western Europe the Promised Land is as far away as ever. And the leaders of the community seem to have no answer. Jewish teaching has become rarified, has lost touch. Jewish teachers seem far more concerned with the esoteric. They have little in common with the down-to-earth, day-to-day, working Jewish peasant of Europe. Poverty and loss of hope are driving them into the ground. But they are still searching for an answer. If there is to be no Jerusalem this year or even next, perhaps it would be better to turn inward to achieve the Promised Land, to take refuge in mysticism. The time is ripe for a new teacher to appear, someone who can offer alternative hope. They are not disappointed.

1700 Israel Ben Eliezer is born in the Ukraine. He earns his living as a lime digger; is poor but content. He has a sweet disposition and loves nature. He believes God dwells in all living things. Holiness (Shekhinah) is within; each person can attain the spiritual heights by

prayer and contemplation, by joy and ecstasy. He infuses new vigour into the downtrodden Jewish masses, imploring all those around him to worship with the heart. He writes no books but his wisdom spreads like a forest fire. He is a sort of holistic medicine man, using plants and herbs to heal the sick and suffering. In fact he is very modern, very revolutionary.

In 1735 Israel performs miraculous cures and becomes known as the Baal Shem Tov (Master of the Good (holy) Name). His wisdom is straightforward and his followers are known as Hassidim (The Pious Ones). They clap their hands, they dance, they sing in the synagogues to welcome the Sabbath. In the midst of prayer the Hassidim sing niggunim, melodies without words, praising the Almighty. A new fervour possesses the Jewish people, especially the Jewish poor. The straight, Establishment rabbis of Poland are concerned; this new phenomenon threatens the old traditions, and even possibly the very foundations of the Jewish faith. They needn't worry. Judaism is always under threat and always survives. The spirit of the Hassidic movement sweeps across Western Europe; it is a shot in the arm to the Jewish people, a sort of rebirth. The idea of serving God through rejoicing transforms the Jewish ethos, and has a profound effect, not only on the Jewish masses, but also on scholars and thinkers. There is a turnaround in the Jewish spirit, a significant move from pessimism to optimism.

Hassidic leaders are stressing the importance of group responsibility. Gradually this new movement is becoming more acceptable. It is certainly more popular than rabbinic Judaism and the Jews in the street perceive themselves in a different light. This new perception helps the Jews look forward again. Suddenly the Land of Israel is not pie in the sky; the dream is not impossible.

Elijah **Ben Solomon** 1720. Known far and wide as the Gaon ("Genius") of Vilna. He is the greatest scholar of this thriving city, known as the "Jerusalem" of Lithuania. The Gaon is brilliant and methodical and very different from the Baal Shem Tov. Elijah's followers are the Mitnagdim (Opposers); conflict between this group and the Hassidim becomes very bitter. The Hassidim believe they are the intermediaries of God. The Gaon believes that each man is responsible to the Almighty and needs no-one to intercede. The battle is furious, the fur hats fly; but eventually these two strands of Judaism decide to end their cold war. Peace is declared.

Naham **of Bratzlav** is a Hassidic Rabbi, born 1722. He publishes his thirteen principles, in Yiddish. Thus this wonderful expressive language, an amalgam of Middle German, Polish, Hebrew and God knows what else, becomes an independent literary language.

Frederick **Hasselquist** 1751. Swedish doctor and naturalist visits the Holy Land, estimates that 4,000 Jews have reached these shores this year.

1771. Still in the Holy Land. The number of synagogues in Safad has risen from seven to thirty.

Let's go back a few years...

*H*askalah (Enlightenment) 1750. This movement is really born in Berlin. Haskalah believes that Jewish emancipation can be best achieved by social conformity with the non-Jewish world. Hebrew must be a living language; Jewish laws and customs must be brought up to date. Haskalah tries to build a bridge between the strict traditionalists and those who believe that assimilation is the only hope for the Jewish people. There are many contradictions and many factions and endless in-fighting amongst its leaders. But Haskalah produces a new sort of Jew, a secular, middle-class person, remaining faithful to his faith, imbued with ideas of Jewish culture, but at the same time living in the reality of modern Europe, aware of the political and social order of the everyday world around him. Or her. But most important of all Haskalah has released a new energy.

From this moment on there is an arrow flying through the air, gathering momentum as it soars towards its inevitable target. The Land of Israel becomes a distinct possibility.

Gotthold Ephriam Lessing 1729-81. Christian playwright. A great champion of the Jewish people. His works are influential amongst German intellectuals. His play Nathan the Wise is a great success. Nathan, the hero, is an intelligent and tolerant Jew.

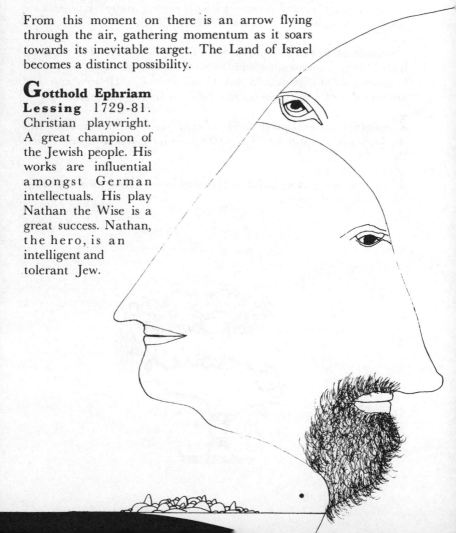

Audiences see Jews in a new light; stereotypes are going down the drain. But Jews are still confined to ghettos. In Frankfurt, Hamburg and Berlin, Jews are still confined and restricted. Only the eldest son of a Jewish family is allowed to marry, and then only after paying out a special tax. Jews still cannot make a decent living, are not allowed to own land outside the ghetto; most of them have to buy and sell second-hand goods. "Plus ca change..."

Yet—hold your horses. A close Jewish friend of Lessing comes to the fore. He will have a marked effect upon the order of things.

Moses Mendelssohn 1729-86. Born a hunchback; he is also ugly and he stammers. Moses is hardly a Greek Adonis to look upon. But he has a brilliant and original mind and enormous energy. Born in Dessau in Germany, the son of a Torah scribe, he moves to Berlin at the age of fourteen, becomes an exceptional scholar with far-ranging interests. His beautiful flowing style of writing plus his mastery of the German language has a great influence on the German Upper Crust, who until now have preferred the French language to their own. He meets Lessing over a game of chess and they become friends for life. This friendship clears the way for Moses, who now has an access card into German intellectual society. He becomes the first German Jew to rise above his brethren who are still confined by the ghetto walls. He becomes a protected, privileged Jew, enjoying freedoms denied his fellow Jews.

The leading writers and scholars of the land fall for his dynamic charm and erudition. But all this doesn't go to his head. His main concern is the emancipation of his brethren. Freedom is in the air, the world is on the brink of change. Moses perceives that a new era of universal enlightenment is about to dawn and he wants the Jews to have part of

the action. He publishes a Hebrew magazine and writes poems, commentaries and articles in Hebrew, but insists that Jews must learn German and understand the world around them; he wants to blow the ghetto wide open, and the ghetto mentality that goes with incarceration. Most of the common folk of Germany are still illiterate, but most of the Jews at least know how to read and write, if only in Hebrew. Under his influence Jewish schools flourish in Berlin and Jewish children receive a far-ranging education that includes vocational training. Moses translates the Five Books of his great biblical namesake into German, but these are printed with Hebrew characters; thus every Jew can read and understand their own culture while broadening their proficiency in the language they must live with.

This new work causes a right fuss but it becomes a main primer, not only for the Jews in Germany, but right across the land mass of Europe. The rabbis shake their heads. This new German bible could be a dangerous innovation. The old way is preferable, safer. But the masses are now eager to learn German, a first important step towards "Enlightenment". Moses Mendelssohn is no assimilationist; despite this overt love for everything German, deep down his one dream is for the survival of the Jewish people, Judaism and all its traditions. No wonderful new laws are passed during his lifetime, but his ideas are taking root, have wide sweeping influence. Jews and Christians are meeting on common ground. No longer are Jews thought to be that different and not worthy of being considered human beings. Hurray, we walk, we talk, we breathe, we think, we have minds, emotions. (Okay, he knew it; but they didn't.)

Moses sets the ball rolling; there is now an impetus for reform and things can never be quite the same. His vision soon causes the ghetto gates to blast open. A Jew is beginning to have a different concept of himself; he can look forward as well as backward. The hunchback has become a giant of Jewish history; a significant link of the cord that stretches from the far dream of Abraham to the now not so impossible dream of returning to the Land of Israel.

Oh yes, one other thing. The old man's grandson, Felix Mendelssohn, becomes a great composer. **Is old Moses proud**? What do you think?

1782   Edict of Tolerance. William Dohm is a Prussian lawyer, a Christian and a good friend of Mendelssohn. Recently the Jews of Alsace have had new punitive laws passed against them. They write to Moses, seeking his help. Moses enlists Dohm who is moved by their request. Dohm drafts a memorandum making a plea for equality and freedom, not only for the Jews of Alsace, but for all the Jews of Western Europe. Joseph II, Emperor of Austria, is in turn moved by this petition and issues his famous Edict of Tolerance. This causes most of the punitive laws to be eased. Jews take a small, but significant leap forward for mankind. But it is a trick: Joseph wants to kill them with kindness.

There has been a Declaration of Independence in America. Britain no longer waives the rules over there. The United States of America becomes the first country where Jews will enjoy total emancipation.

1786 In America the Virginia Statute of Religious Liberty is enacted. It guarantees total freedom of worship. This law influences the Federal constitution of 1787, which is quite categorical: no religious test will ever be required as qualification for any public office.

1790 On the 17th of August the Jews of Newport, Rhode Island send a message of greeting to their President, George Washington, who is visiting the town. Four days later he replies: '... May the Children of the Stock of Abraham, who dwell in this land, continue to merit and enjoy the good will of the other Inhabitants; while every one shall sit in safety under his own vine and fig tree, and there shall be none to make him afraid...'

Thus begins an incredible love affair between the Jewish people and America. The marriage is exceptional and long-lasting.

But...

By 1789 the raging forest fire of revolution is sweeping the world.

July 14th! The Bastille is stormed in Paris. Thus begins one of the most decisive revolutions in history; all Europe is stirring after the long dark night of repression. The French Assembly proclaims the "Declaration of the Rights of Man". Its contents, similar to the American Declaration, underline the new spirit of change. All men are born free and are entitled to equal rights. And that includes Jews.

1790 Bordeaux. All naturalised Jews are granted equality. 1791. A new decree gives Jews the rights and privileges of full citizenship.

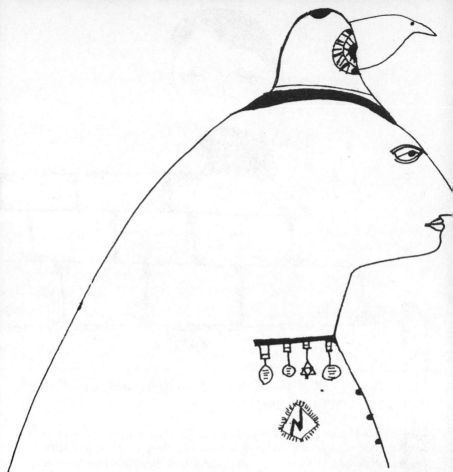

Napoleon Bonaparte 1769-1821. Brilliant soldier, strategist. The New Republic soon becomes involved in war; this young general rises to pre-eminence and takes over the destiny of France. His ambitions recognise no frontiers; his armies surge across Europe, freeing serfs and Jews wherever they go! His code of law, soon to be known as the Napoleonic Code, reinforces new concepts of civil liberties and freedom with legal force. The Emperor is eager to gain the loyalties of the Jews. In 1806 he convenes an Assembly of Jewish leaders, called Sanhedrin (the name of the ancient supreme court in Jerusalem). The object is to formulate an answer to the usual allegation that the Jews are strangers in the lands where they live and, therefore, do not deserve full civil rights. The Assembly of French, German and Italian Jews states that it is the religious duty of Jews to be loyal to the state where they live. Napoleon is a sharp operator; he is devious and ambivalent; people ask "Is he good for the Jews"? Some days he is good, some days he is not so good. But all in all at the end of the day Napoleon does much to hasten Jewish emancipation.

1812 Prussia. All Prussian Jews are emancipated regarding residence, commerce and special taxes.

Heinrich Heine (1797-1856). Great Jewish German poet converts to Christianity; nevertheless he never loses his deep involvement with the Jewish people. His writings reflect this attachment and love. One of his best known poems, Princess Sabbath, describes the life of the Jew and his devotion to his sabbath. On his deathbed a priest chides him for being frivolous and says "May God forgive you." He replies "Why shouldn't he forgive? That's his job." A very Jewish reply. Heine, like many of his fellow German Jews of his time, abandons his faith, but not his god.

Karl Heinrich Marx 1818, is born in Germany. His parents are Jewish but convert to Christianity before he is born. His ideas, contained in his main work, Das Kapital, will have a profound effect upon the world. However, this father of Communism is contemptuous towards the Jews; indeed he is almost anti-semitic, seeing the Jews largely as reactionary and capitalistic.

Others, while far from sharing Marx's kind of views, also believe that Judaism has gone stale. In the year Marx is born the first Reform Synagogue is dedicated in Hamburg, Germany. This Reform Movement, headed by Rabbi Abraham Geiger, introduces German prayers into the service; he also shortens Hebrew prayers which seemed interminable and to have lost their meaning.

Prayers about the Return to Zion and the coming of the Messiah are omitted. The Reform Movement is convinced it can attract modern Jews who are moving with the times and adjusting to modern life.

Russia 1825. Czar Nicholas I comes to the throne. He swipes immediately at the Jews by ordering them to disband their Kahal, their time honoured system of communal self-government. He also wants the Jews to give up their Yiddish language, their religion and their traditions and to be converted to Christianity, by force if necessary. He has further ambitions for his Jewish subjects.

He dreams of a large and powerful army, so he institutes a draft for eighteen-year old boys who will serve for a term of twenty-five years. Jewish boys however get a bonus; they will serve for only thirty-one years—and they are drafted at the age of twelve. Recruiters come and take these children by force. Once in the army they are starved and beaten until they renounce the god of their parents. The Pale of Settlement (the area of Russia to which Jews are confined) is already a going concern, but because of all the intolerable pressures many Jews are forced out of the villages of the Pale and try to scratch a living in the cities. Holy Russia is about as holy as a cesspit. But the Jews, despite all the odds, all the terrible repression, remain loyal to their Judaism.

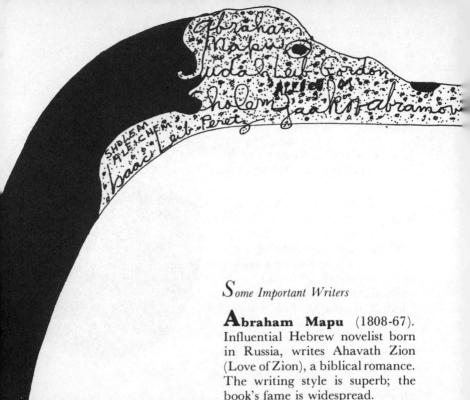

Some Important Writers

Abraham Mapu (1808-67). Influential Hebrew novelist born in Russia, writes Ahavath Zion (Love of Zion), a biblical romance. The writing style is superb; the book's fame is widespread.

Judah Leib Gordon (1830-92). Also born in Russia. Perhaps the greatest 19th century Hebrew poet; he fights fearlessly against some archaic, outmoded Jewish customs and manners, but remains a champion of Jewish traditions as a whole.

Sholem Aleichem (1836-1917, pen-name of Sholem Ya'akov Abramavich). Also born in Russia. It is unbelievable that in these times of such great adversity such giants will arise—to amaze, astound, illuminate. Sholem paints a vibrant picture of the Jews in the Pale; he gives the Yiddish language density, expression and flexibility; he shows the lives, the dreams, of everyday people. He becomes an acknowledged master; his works enter world literature.

Isaac Leib Peretz (1851-1915). Yiddish author, born in Russia. His brilliant Hassidic Tales are written in the language of the common man. Not to be sniffed at.

All these authors are voluble bubbles on the surface of change; they rise out of adversity, express the aspirations of the common folk around them. They enhance their people and help to push them along the inevitable change towards self-enlightenment.

Great Britain. In 1835, David Solomons is elected Sheriff of London. He has fought for the right of Jews to be admitted into public life; the battle has been hard, but eventually he is the first Jew to achieve this high position. Jews are welcome in Britain and are equal, but not as equal as some. They are not allowed in the House of Commons, the British Parliament; neither can they receive academic degrees, nor can they hold public office, with the exception of the office of the Sheriff of London. Mind you the British establishment has got nothing against Jews personally. Some of their best friends . . .

For Parliament, university or public office an oath of affirmation is required, stating "... true faith of a Christian." But Benjamin Disraeli is acceptable. He was born Jewish but, with his parents eye on the main chance, his faith is renounced. When elected Member of Parliament in 1837 he is allowed to take his seat. Many top Jews, like Moses Montefiore and Baron Lionel de Rothschild, are from long-established Jewish families and are accepted by the British Establishment; their loyalty and dedication to the United Kingdom is unquestioned and they have great influence with the Prime Minister. But still the inner sanctum is denied them, and they battle tirelessly for the rules to be changed. Eventually they succeed. Open but not sesame. Rothschild does finally have the pleasure of swearing the oath on a Hebrew Bible, on the faith of a Jew. In 1858 he is the first Jew to become a Member of Parliament. He enters the House of Commons and takes his place.

Lionel de Rothschild and Moses Montefiore belong to two long-standing, well-established Jewish families. They are privileged. You could call them the Upper Crust, but this does not seem to cut them off from the realities of life; they are in touch with what is happening to their brethren, the vast numbers of poor Jews in Britain, struggling for a living. The influence of these two men is widespread and crucial. Montefiore becomes a prodigious traveller, seeking out kings and heads of state, trying to influence them and ease the conditions of their

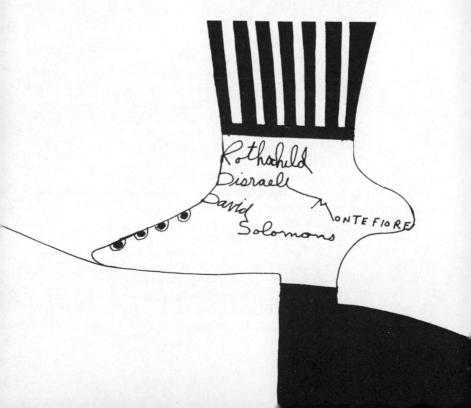

subjects. They go to Syria, where Jews are being tortured and their children imprisoned, falsely accused of murdering a monk. His wife Judith is always with him, and they travel to Egypt which has jurisdiction over Syria. The power of the British government is behind Moses, and he kicks up one hell of a stink. The world soon hears about this latest Damascus outrage. The Egyptian government bows to universal pressure and the Jews of Syria are released and exonerated.

Moses travels to Russia for a face-to-face confrontation with Czar Nicholas I who, as we know, is not exactly a pleasant fellow. Judith, his wife, is with him (where else?) and he presents the Czar with a letter from Queen Victoria. The Czar apparently has a new idea for his Jews; he wants now to force them to leave their homes in the Pale and to be forceably settled in far-off provinces in Unholy Russia. The Czar smiles, nods, as he listens to the persuasive Moses; the Czar is charming, polite and actually permits the Jews to remain in their Pale of Settlement. But the desperation of these poor Jews remains the same. There is little that this traveller can really do to alleviate the suffering of his Russian brethren.

Moses starts to dream. Perhaps there can be another Exodus; perhaps the Jews can really return to the Land of Israel. He visits Palestine six times, bringing support to the Jews already there. He helps to build schools, hospitals, synagogues. He plants vineyards and olive groves, and opens the first experimental agricultural school in the Holy Land, on the outskirts of Jerusalem. He builds a group of homes there, an early nucleus of what will one day be called the New City of Jerusalem. Thus an Upper Crust Jewish, English Gentleman called Montefiore definitely deserves to be remembered and called by his first name. Moses. He is called this for a hundred and one years, during his lifetime, because he lives that long.

The American Connection

Mordechai Noah 1837. This swashbuckling, ex-army officer, politician, playwright, newspaper editor, rallies support to establish a settlement as a city of refuge for the oppressed Jews of the world. He likens himself to his Biblical predecessor and calls his proposed settlement "Ararat"; it is located on Grand Island in the Niagara River. It comes to nothing. But Noah remains obsessed and tries to buy Palestine from the Turks, for hard cash. Christians object to his being Sheriff of New York. "How can a Jew hang Christians?" "What if they deserve it?" replies Noah.

Jews are getting more and more involved in the spirit of the United States. They are becoming expansive, opening out, moving in all directions. The ghetto mentality is beginning to fade. Jews are breathing the air of freedom, indulging in the luxury of hope. They are establishing themselves in the cities, laying down foundations, creating businesses, earning a living. Between 1820 and 1870 the population of the United States rises from ten million to forty million; hundreds of thousands of Jews are pouring in from Europe. But the Jews of America are also on the move, travelling outward into the western expanse. Jews are exploring, pioneering. This is a new art for them; the ability to move freely. Some become pedlars and traders, indeed many do business with the Red Indian trappers. "Him Big Chief Rabbi." Jews are moving to the Midwest, to the West Coast, setting up printing presses, publishing newspapers, opening shops, building synagogues. In the Civil War Jews fight on both sides, loyal to the section of the country they happen to be living in.

1 864 There are twelve thousand Jewish Johnny Rebels serving in the
Confederate Army. Judah Benjamin is called "the brains of the
confederacy". Many, many more Jews are in the Union Army. Seven
Jewish soldiers in the Union ranks are awarded the Congressional
Medal of Honor. Many Jews become active in the anti-slavery
movement. Three Jews from Kansas join John Brown's special army.
Halleluja! And Glory be to them. Rabbis also are speaking out against
slavery; they meet strong opposition. One, Rabbi Einhorn, even has to
flee for his life during the secessionist riots of 1861.

Emma **Lazarus** 1849-87. Jewish poet who is in touch with the
aspirations of millions of people in Europe who long to be free of
persecution and to live in a land of liberty and hope. She writes a poem
that is to become world famous, that symbolises the spirit of America.
This poem, The New Colossus, is engraved on a plaque on the base of
the Statue of Liberty, this giant edifice at the gateway to this new land
of liberty.

"Give me your tired, your poor
Your huddled masses yearning to breathe free
The wretched refuse of your teeming shore
Send these, the homeless, tempest-tost to me.
I lift my lamp beside the golden door."

Emotional words which express a real feeling, a dream that has a potent reality. Emma speaks not only for the oppressed Jews, but for all the huddled masses who dare to hope for change.

By 1880 Jews are fully integrated and well established. They number around 250,000 and many have achieved eminence in American society, excelling in political and commercial life. They do well, particularly in New York. Famous families begin to emerge, described by some as an 'Aristocracy': they occupy Fifth Avenue Mansions, country houses. Famous business names include: **Belmont, Seligman, Kuhn, Loeb and Co., Thalmann and Co., Speyer and Co., Goldman, Sachs and Co.** The American government depends on them when they fight the Confederacy during the Civil War. But soon these long-established, secure, wealthy Jews will be swamped by poor Jews, the huddled masses who are no longer huddling, but seeking freedom from the tyranny of Europe. The story of the Land of Opportunity has got about and now everyone believes that they can enjoy a piece of the action. They are not prepared to put up with Czars any longer.

But not all oppressed Jews will be looking westward, in the direction of Emma Lazarus's America. Some have other ideas. And they start from the roots. . .

The Living Language

"There is a tide in the affairs of man," the poet said. There is certainly a new momentum concerning the Jewish people. But the Jews are still scattered, speak all the tongues under the rainbow. If there is to be a new concept of oneness, then there must be a unifying living language. "When the student's ready, the Master appears," so the old saying goes. In this case two masters appear to ignite a smouldering dream: Hebrew.

Ahad Ha-am ("One of the People") 1856. Pen-name of Asher Ginzburg, born in the Ukraine. He is an ardent champion for the revival of Hebrew as a living language. He also believes that the Land of Israel must once again become the spiritual and cultural centre for the Jewish people. Later he will clash with Herzl, whose emphasis is mainly on political statehood. Ahad Ha'am's work inspires a whole generation of Hebrew writers. One of his disciples becomes the greatest poet in the Hebrew language, Chaim Nahman Bialik.

Eliezer Ben Yehudah is born in Lithuania in 1858. In 1881 he settles in Jerusalem. Another great champion of the Hebrew language. He is a talented linguist and educationalist who has a crucial effect upon Hebrew being adopted and used in everday life, in the new, flowering Jewish homeland. He allows only Hebrew to be spoken at home. Soon his family and friends follow his example. He coins new words for tools, ideas, concepts, all unknown in biblical days. His main publication is a comprehensive dictionary of modern and ancient Hebrew. The language connects and unifies. Now there is a direct continuity, a living link with the past. If the language lives, Israel lives. It is a body rising up.

Over in Central Europe...

1870-1 Germany. Under the Kaiser and his Chancellor, Otto von Bismarck, the Germans have won the Franco-Prussian war. This seems to have gone to their head. They surrender many of their newly-won democratic rights, rights that the Jews have been prominent in fighting for. The Jews become victims of a new wave of persecution that sweeps across Germany and into the rest of Europe. Old superstitions die hard; new obscenities surface. In Germany new harsh laws are being passed against the Jews. They cannot go into the army, civil service or the professions unless they become baptised Christians. Who believed that these battles had long been won? If the Jews once did, they certainly don't now. This new wave of persecution is to have significant repercussions.

Three great men are born at this time, in this part of the world.

Sigmund Freud is born in 1856 in Freiburg, Moravia. He spends most of his life in Vienna. The founder of psychoanalysis changes concepts, revolutionises methods of understanding and dealing with mental conflicts. He considers all religious faiths irrational, and this includes the faith of his fathers. His effect upon modern thinking will be enormous. In his work , Moses and Monotheism, he analyzes anti-semitism.

Martin **Buber** is born in 1878 in Vienna. In 1898 he joins the Zionist movement and later has a significant influence on Zionist ideology. He achieves world-wide fame as a religious philosopher. His most famous work is I and Thou. He has been influenced by Hassidism and interprets this for the Western world. He believes in dialogues between man and God and man and man. He devotes much of his life seeking an understanding with the Arab people.

Albert **Einstein** is born in 1879 in Ulm, Germany. To call him a brilliant physicist is to understate. His Theory of Relativity is an inspired, poetic leap of super-human magnitude; it changes concepts of space and time—his equations will change the world. But Albert is a modest, gentle man, helpful to all. Soon he becomes fearful of his own discoveries, for without Einstein there would be no nuclear bomb. He remains at heart a pacifist. He is always active for Zionism, never forgets that he is a Jew. Many think he is one of the greatest men since the beginning of time. Many years later, after the death of Chaim Weizmann 1952, he will refuse an invitation to stand for election as President of Israel.

Back in Eastern Europe...

1881 Alexander II has ruled for thirty years; he hasn't been too repressive; indeed sometimes he has been quite liberal. But this is not good enough. Times have changed; people will not put up with arbitrary rules any more. Reforms are not widespread enough, not coming fast enough. Workers compare their rights with the rights of the workers in other countries; students discuss, conspire revolution. The time is ripe. Jews join the revolutionary groups believing they must benefit if and when great changes come. During this time many are exiled to Siberia, imprisoned, shot. But they believe this is an unavoidable price to pay for a better future. You can smell revolt in the air. Alexander is afraid. Students now form secret terrorist organizations; bombs are thrown, acts of sabotage are committed. Alexander is assassinated in the streets of St. Petersburg. The rumour spreads: **"The Jews have murdered the Czar."**

Pogrom (Russian word, means destruction). Alexander II is succeeded by his son, Alexander III. He is ruthless and indifferent to the suffering of his people, but his main concern is to stamp out the unrest and revolutionary ideas that are seething in every corner. He looks into history books searching for a device that will work. His day is made. The Jews! They become the usual convenient scapegoat, a very usual device in diverting and utilising the hatred of the masses. If the masses can be made to blame someone else for their misery, they may forget the real cause. And so the machinery of tyranny is switched into top gear. Non-Jewish students, workers, merchants—everyone! anyone! Thousands upon thousands are rounded up, shot or sent to the frozen hell of Siberia. That's just for starters.

Government officials make speeches in public attacking the Jews, inciting the local community to revenge themselves upon the Jews in their midst. Jewish homes are broken into, plundered, destroyed. Jews are shown no mercy; they are attacked, injured, killed. A black plague

of madness sweeps across Russia. Pogroms take place in more than thirty towns in the Ukraine. On Christmas Day 1881 the bells ring out merrily all over Warsaw, a prelude to a devastating attack upon the Jews of the city! In 1883 another series of pogroms occurs: hatred pours on the huddling Jews in villages and towns across Holy Russia. The world is outraged; the Czar doesn't even blink. And so it goes on.

In 1891-92 the Jews are expelled from Moscow. We are talking about thousands of families. We are talking about irrational hatred, about angry, ignorant peasants attacking innocent, despairing people who are gathering up their meagre possessions. We are talking about desperate parents and crying children. The dreaded word Pogrom. It is being whispered in fear, everywhere. The first six years of the twentieth century will witness hundreds of pogroms. Kishinev 1903: forty-five Jews are killed, hundreds injured. Odessa 1905: three hundred Jews murdered, thousands wounded.

The world is outraged. The Czar doesn't blink. He cannot even if he tried. He is dead and his son Nicholas II has succeeded him. But nothing changes. The pogroms go on. The outraged world now tries to lend support. Thousands of Jews manage to flee from Russia, helped by money sent from distant relatives in distant lands, or from donations gathered by Jewish organisations abroad. Thousands make their long way to the New World. A difficult journey, but a picnic in comparison to what they have been through. In a little over ten years half a million Russian Jews will see the Statue of Liberty towering over the Hudson River. But other Jews have other ideas.

Let's go back a few years...

In 1870 the Mikveh Israel Agricultural School is founded near Jaffa. The Jewish community in Jerusalem numbers more than 11,000.

In 1881 Leon Pinsker, Russian-Jewish physician, publishes his pamphlet, Auto-Emancipation. He maintains that the Jews can only emancipate themselves, that they should look to no-one else to grant them freedom. Only by self-help can Jews regain their self-respect and achieve freedom. And this self-respect and this freedom can only be achieved by returning to their ancient homeland, the Land of Israel. The yeast of these ideas begins to have dramatic effect; Jews see themselves in a new light.

1882 Two movements are born this year—Bilu and Hibbat Zion. These movements are junctions pulling together the various trains of thought; they unify actions, lead to realising the ancient dream. These movements together give birth to modern Zionism.

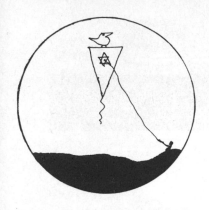

Bilu. The word comprises Hebrew initials of "Bet Ya'acov, Lekhu V'nelkha" from the biblical verse "Let us arise and go." Followers of this movement are as good as their word. They go and they are joined by . . .

Hibbat Zion ("Love of Zion"). The slogan "To Palestine", is their rallying call. Societies are organized in several countries to purchase land in the Land of Israel for settlement by their members. Students respond to the call, but more conservative elements in Russian Jewry and those assimilated Jews in Western Europe oppose the movement. Nevertheless, there is an impetus, a tide that cannot be turned back. The members of both these movements begin a wave of settlement in Palestine.

The First Aliyah 1882-1905. Jewish immigration into Palestine continues steadily. Ever since Ezra the Hebrew word Aliyah refers to the Return of the Jews to the Land of Israel. It literally means "ascent" or "going up". But it also has a religious connection. It means ascent to the reader's desk in the synagogue, referring to the person called up to participate in the reading of the Torah. The Jew honoured thus in the synagogue feels a sense of dedication, inspiration.

The people who make the deserts bloom in this first Aliyah, those who have gone up to Palestine, feel this same dedication and inspiration. But making the desert bloom is a cliche. It sounds easy. A desert is a desert is a desert, a wilderness, a wasteland. A place of rocks that tears your hands to shreds, of sand that clogs your nostrils, a desert burns the eyes, breaks the back, stops your songs.

These pioneers find a barren land. The dream place of Milk and Honey is a land of desert and swamps. Students, professional people from the city, know that the only answer is within themselves. They have to work with their own hands to irrigate the deserts and drain the swamps. Something happens to these Jews, something that has not happened to Jews for thousands of years. Their sweat falls into their own soil; their own soil grows their own trees, their own fruit. This discovery of the land is a discovery of a new purpose for the Jewish people.

These early pioneers fight off hunger, thirst, malaria and attacks from raiding Bedouins, establish the first agricultural settlements in the land. Famous names are now born. Rishon le-Zion ("First In Zion"), Petah Tikvah ("Gate of Hope"), Nes Tziyyonah and Zikhron Ya'akov. And others. And many others. Their orange groves today are witness to their incredible hardship and endeavour and to their absolute determination.

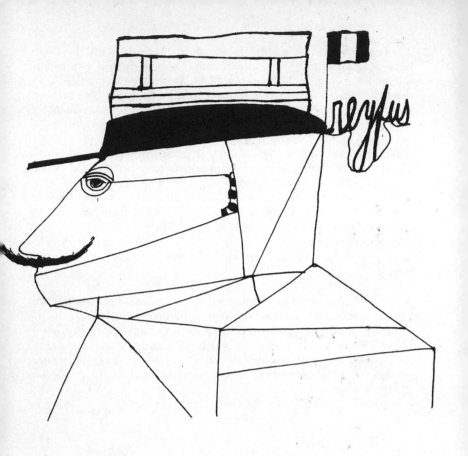

Around this time two other events are taking place in Europe which will have a profound effect on our story. The first was not earth-shattering at the time...

Adolf Hitler 1889. Born in Austria.

The second had immediate impact...

1894 France. Even though French Jews enjoy full civil rights, rights decreed by law, they still find themselves confronted by the same old obscene prejudices. There is an endemic evil streak in La Belle France. Anti-semitism is rife. In October of this year its nauseating head breaks through the surface. Captain Alfred Dreyfus, a Jewish officer on the General Staff, is arrested and charged with espionage. He is accused of giving French military secrets to the Germans, and is tried for high treason. He is sentenced to life imprisonment, in this case exile on the dreaded Devil's Island.

Throughout, Dreyfus protests his innocence; even when he is stripped of his military rank and honours he cries "Long live France! Long live the army!" His conviction sets off a spate of anti-semitic diatribes in the press, but not all Frenchmen are convinced of his guilt. Something is not quite right. Something smells; in fact something positively stinks. There is a suspicion that the incriminating document that Dreyfus is accused of writing could be the handiwork of someone else. No less a person than Emile Zola, the great and respected novelist, takes up the battle for the Jewish officer. He writes a famous article "J Accuse!" This is published in L'Aurore and has an immediate and dramatic effect all round the world. In France all hell breaks loose; there is great tension; all France is divided between those who condemn the Jewish traitor and those who plead his innocence.

The truth finally emerges. Major Ferdinand Esterhazy, the real traitor, walks into the office of a London newspaper and confesses his guilt. The document that convicted Dreyfus was a forgery, designed specially to implicate Dreyfus and thereby divert suspicion away from the real traitor. Despite this confession the French government refuse to re-open the case. Too many high-ups in the Establishment are now involved in the nasty business; re-opening the case would be like opening Pandora's box. Nevertheless, five years later a new government orders a new trial. But again the court condemns Dreyfus; a scapegoat in hand is worth too many in the High Command. But the President of France pardons the Jewish officer. The court's verdict is set aside eventually and Dreyfus is exonerated and reinstated in the army. (You would have thought he has had enough, but he is a loyal Frenchman.)

The trial has revealed a great schism; a rotten questionable element deep in the heart of the French Establishment, a canker eating the soul of France, buried deep beneath the brave slogan "Liberte! Egalite! Fraternite!" The trial of Dreyfus concentrates Jewish minds wonderfully; it is to be a moment of truth, a turning point.

One man is there, reporting the trial for a Viennese newspaper. The trial convinces him that Jews must no longer be a fragmented people, but a nation. This man is...

Theodore Herzl.

Up until this Dreyfus trial Theodore has had little contact with Jewish life and traditions. Indeed, he believes that assimilation is the only way to solve the interminable problem of the persecution of the Jews. He is not a religious man, does not feel any deep affinity with the Jewish soul. He is a philosophical, pragmatic man, influenced more by Spinoza than by God. He has achieved some success as a dramatist and becomes Paris correspondent for the Viennese newspaper, Neue Freie Presse. It is now that the Dreyfus affair explodes on the world and this has a deep and significant effect upon him. Suddenly everything has changed. It is as if all he has done in his life has led him to this point in time. He is deeply shocked and from now on the fate of the Jewish people obsesses him. He sees that the only way that there can be a solution to the Jewish problem is by the establishment of a homeland for the Jewish people. This concept fires him and from now on and until the end of his short life everything that he does is directed towards the realisation of this idea, this ideal.

In 1896 he meets the Sultan of Ottoman Turkey, the Pope, kings, presidents, prime ministers, politicians. He meets everyone, anyone . . . anyone who is prepared to meet him. He argues, discusses endlessly, never ceasing, never tiring, impressing, cajoling, talking, talking. He talks them under the table. He writes a pamphlet, The Jewish State, explaining his ideas. His later novel, Altneuland (Old-New Land), is his vision of a return to Zion. He and his associates call themselves Zionists. They publish a periodical, Die Welt, setting forth their ideas.

1897 Herzl calls the first Zionist Congress in Basle, Switzerland. Here the Zionist movement is officially founded, its basic platform proclaimed: "The establishment of a legally secure homeland in Palestine." From now on he works unceasingly towards achieving this aim, and he dies absurdly young at the age of forty-four. He has accomplished much and from now the launching pad is there. Thousands of people turn up for his funeral. A special correspondent of the London Jewish Chronicle states " . . . It was a wonderful gathering, composed of men and women from many lands. Cheek by jowl with the correctly attired Western Jew one noticed the caftaned heavy-bearded Jew from Galicia, and side by side with the dark-eyed Roumanian was the fair-skinned North German. But on every face was the mark of a huge and lasting sorrow, the look that comes with an irreparable personal loss."

Obviously this is an event of great significance; people have invested all their fervour, all their desperate hopes upon this now dead man. He has become the amalgam that binds all their diversities into one positive strand. The great writer Stefan Zweig is one of the six thousand who follow his funeral cortège on that 7th day of July, 1904. At first it is correct, dignified. Then . . .

" ... a tumult ensued at the cemetery; too many had suddenly stormed to his coffin, crying, sobbing, screaming in a wild explosion of despair. It was almost a riot, a fury. All order was overturned through a sort of elemental, ecstatic mourning such as I have never seen before or since at a funeral. And it was this gigantic outpouring of grief from the depths of millions of souls that caused me to realise for the first time how much passion and hope this lone and lonesome man had borne into the world through the power of a single idea."

All this is now linking up with Eastern Europe...

1905 Revolution in Russia is brutally crushed. More pogroms against the Jews follow.

The Second Aliyah 1905-14. The abortive revolution and the disillusions that follow prove too much for many Jews. It is the catalyst that makes many of them turn their back on Russia for ever. Some 35,000 to 40,000 depart for Palestine, most of them with socialist ideals, transferring their burning zeal to this new-old land and planning to turn it into a socialist paradise.

But not everything in the Garden of Eden is lovely. These pioneers of Labour Zionism may arrive with high hopes, but the reality is something else. Most of them complain of lack of jobs or exhaustion or the sheer harshness of their existence. In Petah Tikvah the already established capitalistic planters are antagonistic, hostile. The farmers not only dislike the immigrants' lack of experience, they are also concerned about their new socialist theories. The Orange Growers

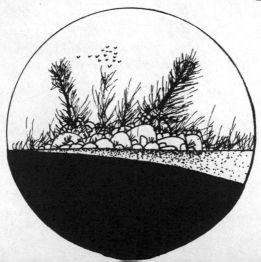

Journal warns... "They want power, economic and social dictatorship over the agricultural domain and those who own it."

In the face of this antipathy the new immigrants wander from place to place, often in rags, many at the point of collapse from sheer lack of food. David Ben Gurion, a nineteen year old former student, gets malaria, almost dies. A doctor urges him to return, but quick, to Europe. Just as well he takes no notice. Who would have been the first Prime Minister forty years later? This socialist strand, this emphasis upon the need to devote your labour, your own sweat, to developing the land cannot be underestimated. These youthful visionaries share an ideal with the great Hebrew poet, Bialik, who understands the despair of a people distanced from their own soil:

"Not my hands formed you, O ears of corn,

Nor my hands fostered your growth;

Not I have spent my strength here,

Nor I will enjoy your harvest!"

The Tolstoyan dream is linked with Karl Marx and the prophets of the Bible.

In 1909 Tel Aviv is founded on the sand dunes of Jaffa. The first felafel seller sets up shop. Kibbutz Degania is also established.

1914 The First World War breaks out. The world goes mad, but for the Jews what's new? Irrational hatred and violence have been everyday occurences for the Jew for thousands of years. Now carnage is on a grand scale. Now we have the Black Death, the Great Pogrom, the Hill of Darkness all rolled into one; the great Moloch is swallowing millions of young lives. Jews are in the thick of it, in all countries, defending their own particular native land, singing patriotic songs of this land, dying for a cause they believe is their own. Terrible battles take place, not only in France and Belgium, but also along the borders of Russia, right through the Pale of Settlement. The Czar is paranoid, he suspects the Jews of disloyalty. Apart from their suffering caused by the war, thousands are deported to a living death in Siberia. The Turks are allies of the Germans and Austrians. They control Palestine, but they fear the Jews who have settled there, know that these settlers feel an affinity with Great Britain and the Allied cause. The Turkish government deports and exiles some 11,000 Palestinian Jews, David Ben Gurion and Yitzhak Ben Zvi (later to become Israel's second President) among them.

Sykes-Picot Treaty (1916). Anglo-French secret agreement provides for the dismemberment of the Turkish Empire. Palestine is to be broken up and shared between the British, French and Russians. The Zionist leaders are not happy; they believe this will expose the Jewish population to constant power struggles.

Dr **Chaim Weizmann** (born Pinsk, Russia, 1874) is a brilliant chemist who now lives in England. During this World War there is a serious shortage of acetone, a material essential for the manufacture of explosives. Dr. Weizmann discovers a new formula for making this stuff; this discovery in turn makes a significant contribution to the Allied cause. The British feel they owe Weizmann a favour, ask him to name his price, but he refuses payment. Instead he requests that if Britain gains control of Palestine the Jewish people should be given special consideration. He pleads for free and unrestricted immigration into Palestine once the Turks are defeated and the war won. The British already look with favour on Jewish settlement in Palestine. But the British motives are perhaps more pragmatic than altruistic: they know that the Jews are not madly in love with the Turks in this vitally strategic part of the world, and ultimately the Jews can only help the British. It will also encourage American and Russian Jews to get their governments to support the British. On the other hand the British attitude is not entirely cynical. There are many members of the British government who genuinely sympathise with the Zionists and their heroic attempts at turning the land into a living state. Many people in Great Britain see Jews as the "The People of the Book".

November the 2nd 1917 proves to be a momentous day in an eventful, fateful year. James Balfour, the British Foreign Secretary, sends a letter to Lord Walter Rothschild:

"His Majesty's Government view with favour the establishment in Palestine of a national home for the Jewish people, and will use their best endeavours to facilitate the achievement of this object..."

Jews all over the world rejoice. An important battle has been won. But the battle in Palestine still continues and there is bitter fighting. A Jewish Legion is formed to fight alongside the British, under the command of the British General, Lord Allenby. Among the recruits is one David Ben Gurion.

Nili Spies. (Nili = initials of Hebrew phrase meaning "The eternity of Israel shall not deceive.") Aaron Aronsohn and his sister, Sarah (said to be a friend of T.E. Lawrence), are part of the pro-British and anti-Turkish underground movement working for General Allenby, commander of the British forces. They transmit information to British warships off the Palestinian coast. They help the Allied cause considerably. But they are caught, tortured and executed.

1917 General Allenby enters Jerusalem and ends Ottoman rule.

The Russian Revolution 1917. The Russian people have finally had enough. The Czar is deposed and executed. The provisional government nullifies all anti-Jewish decrees and for a time Jews believe a new age is about to dawn. There are many Jews prominent in the Kerensky regime and later in the Bolshevik Revolution. Anti-semitism becomes a criminal offence. If you could only legislate away deep, ingrained, irrational hatred. It is deep-rooted in the Russian ethos, as potent as the icons. However, they try. Prominent Jews in the Bolshevik revolution include Zinoviev, Sverdlov and Leon Trotsky. Trotsky is a genius. He organises the Red Army, but he feels no affinity with any specific Jewish cause; indeed, he is antagonistic toward Judaism. Later, however, he starts to feel some sympathy for Jewish nationalism; later still, he falls victim to Stalin. He will be murdered in Mexico in 1940 by an ice-pick being stabbed into his skull several times.

For the Jews disillusion sets in very soon after the Revolution. Hebrew is discouraged and Zionism proscribed. At first the Jews are allowed to maintain their own traditions, their language and culture, but even this policy is drastically changed. Religious and cultural freedom will be denied them. Dreams of Jerusalem are forbidden; only dreams of a bright Red Dawn are allowed. Despite this, Jews will continue to dream in secret. Maybe one day the Red Sea will open up again.

Meantime, two Russian-born Jews are making their impact in Palestine.

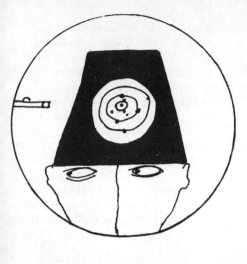

Vladimir Jabotinsky is a writer and orator. He advocates the setting up of Jewish regiments to fight the Turks. This leads to the establishment of the Zion Mule Corps. Later, in opposition to official Zionism, he will be one of the founders of Zionist Revisionism, antecedent of the present-day Herut party.

Joseph Trumpeldor is a kind of Zionist buccaneer. Loses an arm fighting the Japanese in 1904. Settles in Palestine. A colleague of Jabotinsky, he helps to set up the Zion Mule Corps. Later in 1920 he will be killed defending Tel Hai, an early settlement in Upper Galilee.

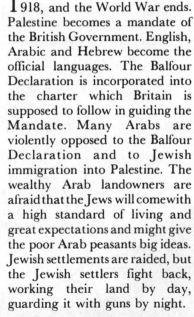

1918, and the World War ends. Palestine becomes a mandate of the British Government. English, Arabic and Hebrew become the official languages. The Balfour Declaration is incorporated into the charter which Britain is supposed to follow in guiding the Mandate. Many Arabs are violently opposed to the Balfour Declaration and to Jewish immigration into Palestine. The wealthy Arab landowners are afraid that the Jews will come with a high standard of living and great expectations and might give the poor Arab peasants big ideas. Jewish settlements are raided, but the Jewish settlers fight back, working their land by day, guarding it with guns by night.

Things are also happening on the other side of the Atlantic...

In the U.S.A. Jews are becoming fully assimilated. Most are armchair Zionists; they dig into their pockets, but not into the earth. There are about four million Jews in the U.S.A. now. One quarter of a million Jewish men serve in the U.S. Army during this war. 3,500 are killed. But the Jews are doing well, moving out of the downtown areas; they are moving away from tailoring, peddling. They are established right across the fabric of American life. Some who make it to the top become famous philanthopists. **Schiff, Warburg, Rosenwald, Strauss, Guggenheim**! They give millions to Jewish and non-Jewish organisations. **Julius Rosenwald** alone helps establish 5,300 schools throughout the U.S.A. for blacks. Jews are also prominent in the trade union movement. **Samuel Gompers** is one of the founders of the American Federation of Labor. **Sidney Hillman** is one of the founders of the Amalgamated Clothing Workers. **Ben Shahn** is a painter with great social commitment; he will vividly bring to life on canvas the agonizing trial of the famous anarchists Sacco and Vansetti. Through both their earlier suffering in Europe and their present social and political awareness Jews are helping to bring social consciousness to the U.S.A. You name it, they are making it right across the board, right across the land.

Doctors. Lawyers. Dentists. Psychiatrists. Actors. Performers. They are moving into movies, show business. Women are busy becoming Jewish American mothers. They are so proud; they are crying tears of joy because their sons have done so well. What do you do for aggravation when you have a boy called **Edward G. Robinson, Irving Berlin, Eddie Cantor, Jascha Heifetz, Ben Hecht, Clifford Odets, Bugsy Segal**?

If only things were that simple . . .

In America anti-semitism is growing. The Ku Klux Klan that advocates white Protestant supremacy gains an estimated four to five million members. Many politicians seeking office in the South, but also in Oregon, Maine and Indiana, win elections with the backing of the Klan. Henry Ford, the great genius of the motor car, owns a

newspaper called The Dearborn Independent. This publishes sections of the The Protocols of the Elders of Zion, which purports to reveal a Jewish plot, created by a Jewish secret society, to take over the world. This document is a scurrilous anti-semitic fabrication whose origins go back to 19th century Russia. Every so often the sewers are opened and the stench of the Middle Ages becomes unbearable. Henry Ford has re-opened the sewers again. A year later, in 1921, Philip Graves, Constantinople correspondent of the London Times, proves that these Protocols are a clumsily plagiarized satire created to ridicule Napoleon III. The credibility of these Protocols is destroyed. Years later, in 1927, Henry Ford apologises, calls Jews his "fellow men and brothers". He begs forgiveness. Despite the Protocols being proved a complete fabrication they are later used by the Nazis as propaganda and later still by the Arabs, being spewed up yet again and distributed widely in Arab and African countries.

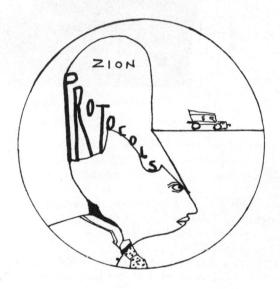

1919. Peace Conference at Versailles. France is ravaged and exhausted by the bloody war; Germany and Austria lose their empires, become republics. Russia is now a communist dictatorship. The world has changed rather drastically. This conference extracts a high price from Germany. To the victors the spoils. Most people agree at a later stage that the price is too high. A price that will be economically disastrous for the German people and will destabilise a people who are already punchdrunk from the ruinous war; and this will in turn lead to one of the greatest human cataclysms the world will ever know.

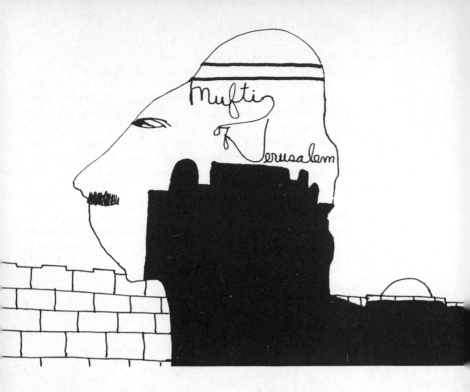

Chaim Weizmann meets King Feisal of Syria in Paris. The Arab king is at first sympathetic to the Zionist cause and they reach an agreement on mutual aid between Jews and Arabs.

Third Aliyah now begins. Youthful elements predominate. This new wave of immigration into Palestine consists mainly of Jews who are leaving Poland and Russia after the Revolution.

Sir Herbert Samuel, the first professing Jew to hold Cabinet office in a British government, is appointed High Commissioner in Palestine in 1920.

Histadrut (The General Federation of Workers in Israel) is established to build up a Jewish labour economy and to develop a network of social institutions to cater for the Jewish working class. Its economic activity becomes part of the bedrock of Jewish society, part of the foundation of the evolving Jewish Palestine. Its influence is widespread, involved in health insurance, vocational schools, cultural centres, theatre. It also publishes newspapers. Later its membership will also include Arabs. Histadrut's influence will become a permanent and significant element of the future Jewish state.

Haganah (Hebrew: "Defence"). This clandestine organisation is set up for the purpose of Jewish self-defence. It replaces Hashomer ("The Watchman"), the earlier self-defence group, set up in 1909.

1921 Sir Herbert Samuel, in less than infinite wisdom, appoints one Haj Mohammed Amin El Husseini as Mufti of Jerusalem. This Grand Mufti is far from grand and not altogether kosher. From now on he causes no end of trouble, organising disturbances and violence against the Jews. Later the British will expel their Mufti. But in exile he becomes acquainted with all sorts of dubious characters. In Iraq he participates in a pro-Axis (Germany-Italy) coup. Finally during World War II he finds his own true love, Herr Adolf Hitler. Mufti is largely responsible for the liquidation of the Jews in the Moslem areas of Bosnia.

But despite continuing and increasing Arab attacks, Jewish settlements continue to develop. The Arabs relentlessly try to stop the inevitable course of events—a momentum towards Palestine. It is unstoppable. During the next ten years the Jewish population will reach 160,000. By 1933 there will be 250,000 Jews in the land and by 1939 half a million. 150 settlements will be established, both collective and conventional farm villages (Kibbutzim and Moshavim).

Cultural life abounds in burgeoning cities, publishing houses flourish, people queue outside cinemas, theatres. And who knows? . . . there may even be one or two houses of ill repute; after all, Jews are only human. People argue in Hebrew on pavements, outside cafes, and everywhere people talk and sing and shout. You can't hear yourself speak, but then what can you expect from a Jewish gathering? Besides, when Jews feel at home they want to be heard.

Emir Abdullah supported Great Britain during the Great War. Now he invades Eastern Palestine and reaches Amman. Winston Churchill meets him in Jerusalem and proposes to Abdullah that Transjordan become an integral part of Britain's Palestine Mandate but not part of the Jewish Homeland as envisaged by Balfour. Churchill is asked to clarify the British position by Herbert Samuel, the High Commissioner in Palestine. Churchill appears ambivalent. During World War II he will maintain his restrictive policy in Palestine, yet there is no doubt of his pro-Jewish attitude throughout his long career. Indeed, he is one of the first politicians in Britain to insist upon the recognition of the State of Israel.

1922 Churchill's proposal viz a viz the Mandate is now official policy, laid down in the White Paper, under Churchill's direction, drawn up by Sir Herbert Samuel and published on July 1st. This becomes the official interpretation of the British Mandate in Palestine. The area east of the River Jordan becomes Trans-Jordan and is taken out of the area designated in the Balfour Declaration. It is closed to Jewish settlement. This is politics. Countries are being carved up. And this is the Middle East where wheeling and dealing is part of everyday life. Nothing is straightforward. Emir Abdullah, like Churchill, is an ambiguous man. He seems to have a moderate attitude towards Zionism and negotiates with Chaim Weizmann. But later he will invade Israel (1948) and will proclaim himself ruler of the Hashemite Kingdom of Jordan. But he will still try to reach an understanding with Israel which will cost him dearly. He will be assassinated in Jerusalem, probably at the behest of the Grand Mufti of Jerusalem. Perhaps Abdullah sees into the future, knows that there can be no complete peace in the Middle East until there is peace between those close relatives, the Arabs and the Jews.

Not very far away...

Germany. Many Jews are playing a prominent role in the Weimar Republic. Germany is trying to pick itself up after a war that has totally depleted its resources and spirit. German Jews are prominent in the administration and are also involved in all walks of life—the arts, the sciences, education, banking, business. It looks as if a new Golden Age is about to dawn, for the Jews and for the rest of Germany. Jews are proud of their German heritage. Many call themselves "Germans first, Jews second". Jewish thinkers are thinking; new theories about God, the universe and the meaning of man abound; theatre is exciting, it is astringent, sardonic, full of caustic wit; new methods of production are being created. Architecture is undergoing a marvellous revolution. Painters are making a fantastic impact upon the world. The world of music is bursting with new experimental techniques.

But all these remarkable achievements will soon be undermined. Terrible problems are just surfacing. Returning soldiers, humiliated in defeat, are not the conquering Teutonic heroes of myth, but a disgruntled rabble who feel betrayed and now have to scratch for a living. The stridency of German nationalism has turned sour; national unity had only ever been skin deep, had had no integral roots before

Bismark. There seems to be a fatal flaw in the diamond and no amount of surface polish can disguise this fact; this flaw is volatile and dangerous. Nationalism plus humiliation is a potent compost for growing hatred. Now there are new groupings—former army officers conspire with improverished aristocrats. They want to avenge their recent defeat; they yearn for the old ways under the Kaiser, for the old dream of Wodin, their old Teutonic god, exemplified by the orgiastic, triumphant music of Wagner. Reality is not bearable, so they indulge in dreams of power and glory, forever and ever German. They have lost their glorious empire, their self-esteem; their world is being eroded, undermined by foreigners who dare to think of themselves as Germans. The Jews are the cause of their misfortune. These dark rumbling hatreds are the other side of the coin to the Weimar Republic.

Walter Rathenau is the brilliant Minister of Foreign Affairs in the government. He is also a Jew. Rathenau is an enlightened man who seeks to improve relations with France. He is an idealist who wants to replace hatred with reason. He is accepted all over the world as a political giant; and he is deeply respected. In a great speech in Genoa on May 19th, 1922, he ends with the famous cry of Petrarch "Pace-Pace-Pace!" One month later, leaving his home, on his way to the Foreign Office, he is assassinated by a hail of bullets and hand grenades. Reactionaries have committed an act of terror—an augury for the terrible future.

Back in Palestine...

Fourth Aliyah now begins. Most of these newcomers are from Poland; they are mainly middle class. Just as well, because in America a bill is passed in Congress drastically curtailing immigration into the United States from Eastern and Southern Europe. (Immigrants from England and Germanic countries still welcome.)

Haifa, Palestine. The Technion ('Israel Institute of Technology') opens in 1924. And in 1925 the Hebrew University is officially opened in Jerusalem by Lord Balfour on Mount Scopus. There is a relatively peaceful period at the moment. This is shattered by...

...an incident at the Western Wall in Jerusalem in 1929. This sparks off a wave of violence all over Palestine. The Mufti claims that the Jews have designs upon the Moslem holy places in Jerusalem. On August 23rd an Arab mob attack Jews in the Golden City; these attacks are repeated the following day. Now the violence spreads all over the country. In Hebron Arabs massacre seventy men and women; there are attacks in Tel Aviv and on the Jews in Haifa; in Safad eighteen are killed and many wounded. There are attacks on settlements up and down the country; defenders hold out against incredible odds. After a week of this bloody attrition large detachments of British troops have to be brought in. Order is restored—for the time being.

Why was all this happening?

The early Jewish settlers in the Yishuv (the Jewish community in Palestine) are mainly idealistic and impoverished, they work with their hands, they live frugally. In many respects this makes them readily acceptable to the local Arabs. They pose no threat. For the fellahin (peasants) life has not changed much for thousands of years; they work with primitive tools, for a pittance. The Mufti and the Arab landowners fear that the expectations of the poor peasants will change with these Jews in their midst. And the Jewish settlers all the while are making progress. Previously unworked land is now producing

everything that can grow. And the great divide is under way. The impoverished Jewish settlers are becoming more prosperous; now the poor Arab, desperate in his poverty, has an object outside himself to turn his anger against. These riots will continue and the British will come under pressure to rescind the Balfour Declaration. There will be much argy-bargy and murky business in the next few years. The British response to renewed Arab pressure will be one of panic, causing them to speak with forked tongue. They will appease the Arabs by whittling away their commitment as set out in the Balfour Declaration, and at the same time they will try to reassure the Jews that nothing has changed. The British become quite adept at the appeasement business; they are rehearsing perhaps for the big show that opens in Munich in the not too distant future.

1931 The Jewish response in Palestine to the waffling British is the immediate strengthening of Haganah, the self-defence organisation. Now there is a split in the ranks of this underground, a growing people's army. The left-wing and the right-wing fall out (when didn't they?). The Irgun Zva Le'umi (right-wing) is thus founded. This split will have wide repercussions in a few years.

Events elsewhere, though, are taking on a momentum of their own...

By 1933 the world is engulfed in economic depression. The consequences are deep and wide. Cracks appear in structures that seemed secure. Political and social earthquakes follow, shaking the foundations of the U.S.A. and Europe. The whole fabric of civilisation will be ripped apart; sanity will run away and the world will explode. The Jews will be at the centre of the explosion.

Adolf Hitler has been installed as Chanceller of Germany. He has absolute control. An Irish poet, William Butler Yeats, has written some prophetic words. "Things fall apart, the centre cannot hold."

The centre of Germany is no more; the benign Weimar Republic has been ripped apart. The Great Depression has decimated Germany, both morally and physically. Unemployment and inflation soar; social unrest has led to riots, armed clashes, a desperate struggle and confrontation between the Right and the Left. There has been bloodshed and murder. The country has been on the abyss, you can smell the threat of civil war. Hitler has appeared, but not out of a puff of smoke. He comes from somewhere; he must answer some kind of distorted need; he must echo some of the deep-rooted sentiments. In fact he springs from the bedrock of German mythology, with its dreams of greatness and glory. He promises something the German people want to hear. He will take away their indecision, their fear; he will give the German people back their self-respect.

At this point nobody asks the price that has to be paid; they hear what they long to hear. The German nation will arise and shake the world and make all other nations tremble. Germans are the master race, superior to all other nations; they will lead the world and wipe out all inferior beings. Germany has been bled for too long by foreigners surrounding them and by foreigners in their midst. The Jew. Particularly the Jews. It is all in Mein Kampf. His book. To know where he stands and what he hopes to do is all set down in the book he wrote in Landsberg-am-Lech, a prison fortress where he had been sentenced for treason. His hatred of the Jews is an overwhelming obsession. "Gradually I began to hate them. I was transformed from a weakly world citizen to a fanatical anti-semite." His obscene diatribes worm their way right through his book. It is all there in black and white, his philosophy, his hatred, his intentions. He makes terrible promises and he is a man of his word. In prison he has dreamed of power and now the dream has come true. But it will be a nightmare for the rest of the world, and especially for the Jews. Now he has achieved supreme power.

The impossible has become possible.

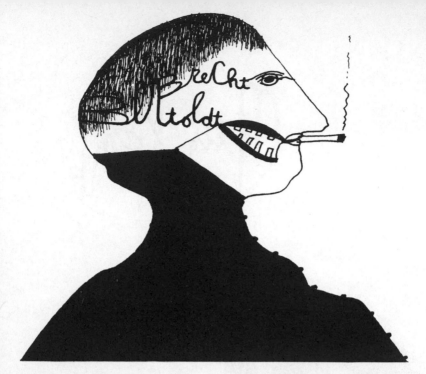

"Don't worry!" people reassure each other. "These are modern times. Germany has to deal with other nations! Germany will come to her senses. When you seek power you make all sorts of wild statements; but when you are in charge of a modern state you have to be realistic and modify your wild ideas." Nobody takes Hitler seriously at first; even most German people laugh at his theories. We all want to be reassured; to believe what we want to believe. We do not want to hear the slow bell tolling; we don't want to be reminded of the words of the great English poet: ".... do not send to know for whom the bell tolls. It tolls for thee."

There is another poet, a left-wing German who has to flee for his life. Bertoldt Brecht's words still reverberate. "He who is an optimist hasn't yet heard the bad news." But there are now few optimists left in Germany. Or in the rest of the world.

Hitler's rise to power has an immediate impact upon the Jews. The reign of terror begins. Germany is a land of fear; concentration camps are being set up. Anti-semitism is the official creed; hate propaganda depicting Jews as inferior people is published, broadcast. Traditional anti-semitic stereotypes are once again trundled out—but this time the obscenities are the policy of the state. The whole of Germany is infected with the madness. The first anti-Jewish riots take place in Berlin; the Nazi boycott of Jewish shops is under way.

Palestine. Fifth Aliyah. In 1931 there were 190,000 Jews in this country. The rise of Hitler and the persecutions in Germany will have a considerable effect upon immigration. Between 1933 and 1936 there will be a flood of Jews seeking sanctuary. More than 164,000 will arrive during this period. Most of them come legally, but thousands come as "illegal" immigrants. The British have imposed restrictions on Jewish immigration and land purchase, but the Jews of the Yishuv question the British interpretation of the Mandate; they regard the British attitude as arbitrary.

One would have thought that with all this horror breaking out in the world the Jews would come together, sort out their differences and present a united front. One would have thought and one would have been wrong. From the outside a family may seem peaceful, cohesive; from within all hell is breaking loose. The Revisionist movement in Palestine steps up its activities against "the Left". There is bitter division in the two camps and this reaches a climax in June, 1933, when Chaim Arlosoroff, one of the leaders of the labour movement, is murdered by unknown assailants on a Tel Aviv seashore. The left accuse the right of the murder. Some members of the Revisionist movement are tried but are eventually acquitted. The controversy will continue for more than fifty years.

Nuremberg, Germany. 1935. The persecution of the Jews has become widespread and accepted by the German people, but they have had no authoritative backing by law. On September 15th, 1935 all this is changed. Laws are approved by the Reichstag at Nuremberg which will give legal approval for racial hatred. Now you are legally permitted to persecute Jews, which is just as well for the nice, law-abiding German citizen. If you want to beat up an old Jew or smash a shop window it helps to know that the law is on your side.

The new laws are extremely punitive and everything is exact and codified and thorough. Jews are excluded from German citizenship; extra-marital relations between Jews and non-Jews are strictly forbidden; marriage between Jews and non-Jews is strictly forbidden. Jews are forbidden to employ non-Jewish servants; Jews are forbidden to hoist or wave a German flag (would any want to at this stage?). A Jew is defined as someone with at least two Jewish grandparents. A series of supplementary decrees place Jews outside German law and exclude them from economic life.

We are now back to the dark ages—and in the no-man's land beyond. The way to utter insanity is now paved with legislation.

1 936 Meantime, the Spanish Civil War breaks out. This war epitomises the sharp differences between good and evil. Spain, in its death throes, is cynically used by the superpowers to test out their strategies and their weapons of death. The carnage is horrendous; brother taking up arms against brother, and killing the other. The world watches, transfixed with horror, as the door is slammed against hope. This terrible war, however, is but an overture to the dreadful Apocalyptic Symphony that is to follow. Many Jews throughout the world rally to the Republican call and serve with the International Brigade against the Fascists. They see this as a last chance to save the world.

1936 In the same year the Arab Revolt begins. April 19th, riots break out in Jaffa. Two Jews are murdered in Tel Aviv by Arab terrorists. The funeral turns out to be a demonstration which leads to the murder of two Arabs. And so it goes on. Sixteen Jews are murdered; property is ransacked, burned, many wounded. The Arabs announce a general strike. An Arab committee, headed by the Grand Mufti, demands the end of Jewish immigration and the prohibition of land being transferred to Jewish ownership; it calls for the establishment of a "national representative government". This is the beginning of three years of public disorder and violence. The general strike lasts for six months. It ends in October, but the violence continues. Jewish settlements and convoys are attacked by armed bands; these attacks are supported by the Arab population and by the clandestine assistance of senior Arab officials and police officers. The Arabs also attack British police and army detachments, try to organise their various terrorist bands into a cohesive group. This attempt fails.

Meanwhile, the Jews have found a new champion. Or perhaps he has found the Jews. He is a non-Jew, a small, intense British army officer.

Charles Orde Wingate This soldier has deep idiosyncratic convictions. Wingate is a keen student of the Bible and believes that the Jews are the "People of the Book", who have a mission to re-establish their homeland in Palestine. He is even more of a Zionist than some of the Jews he commands. He sets up Special Night Squads within the Haganah; he commands enormous respect from his volunteers who are devoted to him. Wingate is a brilliant strategist who achieves much success against the Arabs. He remains an ardent Zionist throughout his distinguished career, an outstanding friend of the Jews until the day he is killed in the forthcoming war.

Haganah set up special stockade and tower settlements during the continuing Arab attacks. The British bring in large military forces to meet the Arab threat, using tanks and aircraft. The British government seem unwilling to meet Arab demands; but they send out a Royal Commission to institute an enquiry, looking into all the problems of this highly volatile land. This Commission is headed by Lord Peel. The general strike has ended but violence seethes just below the surface. The Commission hears a host of witnesses.

The Peel Commission publishes its findings in July 1937. There is a revolutionary proposal to partition Palestine into two states. A Jewish state would consist of the whole of Galilee, and the coastal strip down to the south of Rehovot. The Arab state would comprise Samaria, Judea, the Negev, Jerusalem and environs, linked to the coast at Jaffa by a corridor that will remain in British hands; this is for the purpose of supervising the Holy Places. The British government announces that it is ready to implement the Commission's findings but the Jews and the

Arabs are not so sure; opinions are sharply divided amongst themselves. Weizmann, Ben Gurion and Shertok (Sharett) are in favour; Jabotinsky and co. are definitely opposed. In the Arab camps Emir Abdullah favours partition, hoping to incorporate the Arab portion into his kingdom and thereby create a huge Arab state which would co-operate with the Jewish State. The Arab High Committee are dead against. In September there are renewed disturbances. The British District Commissioner in Galilee is murdered by Arabs. The British hit back, disband the Arab High Committee, arresting its leaders and sending them packing into exile on the Seychelles Islands. But the Grand Mufti is slippery; he escapes the net, turns up in Syria and continues to direct his campaign of terror from there.

And the reign of terror continues unabated. 415 Jews are murdered by terrorists between 1937 and 1939. Despite this, the terrorists fail to make any real impact upon Jewish life in Palestine; with few exceptions they do not break into Jewish towns or villages.

By the summer of 1938 the Arab revolt reaches its climax. Terrorists capture police stations and break into Arab towns. For a brief spell in October they hold the Old City of Jerusalem (except the Jewish Quarter). The British drive them out again. The British now concentrate large forces against the Arabs, using 16,000 troops to combat the terrorists. The Arab population gets fed up with the perpetual murder and blackmail and set up "peace-bands" to fight the terrorists. The revolt peters out. By the spring of 1939 it will have come to an end.

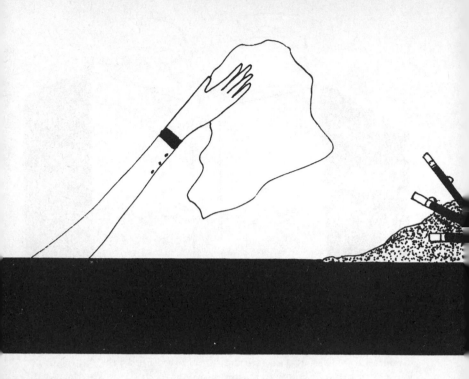

Events begin to link up...

A ppeasement 1938. There is something rotten in the state of Britain; many members of the Establishment openly want to do a deal with Adolf Hitler, even though it is obvious he is after world conquest. Lady Astor and her cronies in The Times, and even some members of the government, seem eager to help Hitler swallow his latest morsel, Czechoslovakia. Mr. Neville Chamberlain, the British Prime Minister, flies to Hitler's home in Berchtesgarden and does a deal with the Fuehrer; then he comes home, waving a piece of paper, the treaty he has signed with the master of death: "I believe it is peace for our time," he says. Thus Czechoslovakia is absorbed into the Third Reich and the curtain goes up on the terrible tragedy of our time (of all time ... so far!). The pact signed between Britain, France and Germany becomes known as the Munich Agreement, and this agreement becomes a byword for appeasement. Hitler now knows he can get away with anything.

The fate of the Jews of Europe is sealed.

Germany. November 9-10th, 1938: This night is known as Kristallnacht, because of the crystal spinters of glass from the shattered windows of synagogues all over Germany. On this night of terror more than two hundred synagogues are destroyed. Fire and looting, devastation and plunder; the mobs of Germany are on the rampage. More than two thousand Jews are murdered in concentration camps.

Even in Palestine, appeasement is in the air. Now the British decide they they must appease the Arabs, lest they join Britain's enemies in the event of a world war. On November 9th they announce the abandonment of the partition plan, and invite Jewish and Arab leaders to a round table conference in London. The Arabs refuse to sit down with the Jews, so in fact there are two separate conferences. There is no agreement whatsoever at these two lots of talks.

1939 Malcolm MacDonald, the British Colonial Secretary, publishes a new White Paper. This is almost total capitulation to Arab demands. Jewish immigration into Palestine is to be restricted to 10,000 a year for five years; after this time any further Jewish influx into the Holy Land will depend upon Arab consent. The sale of land to Jews is to be severely restricted.

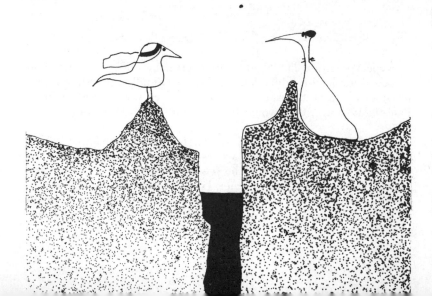

As a special gesture 25,000 additional certificates of immigration will be issued for Jewish refugees from Europe. Finally the White Paper provides for the establishment, within ten years, of an independent Palestinian state which would have strong links with Britain.

The British government immediately applies the White Paper policy. This is a complete turnabout and is against anything that Balfour envisaged in his Declaration. The Jews are furious and on the day the paper is published they call a general strike. Mass demonstrations take place in Jewish towns and villages. Haganah form a special unit to attack telephone lines, railroads and other government installations.

The Arabs too are dissatisfied. They don't think the British have gone far enough; they want to see a total end to immigration. Indeed, they would like to see another Exodus.

The three years of the Arab revolt have been a testing time for the Jews. Yet, despite all the uncertainty, the Jewish economy is getting stronger. The Yishuv is now able to supply its own vegetables, fruit, eggs and much other food. There is a spectacular growth in the establishment of agricultural settlements. The idea of "Jewish labour" has come to fruition. Jews are no longer only scholars and merchants, doctors and lawyers. Jews are working in the ports and in the quarries; it is now acceptable and expected that Jews are working across the whole spectrum of employment.

For the Jews this is a revolutionary achievement. The Arabs, though, have other concerns. Many are now throwing in their lot with Nazi Germany. They follow the Grand Mufti who decrees that the Third Reich is their best bet for getting rid of the Jews. But despite all the Arab hatred and all the restrictions imposed by the British, immigrants are still pouring in. Sixty thousand legal and "illegal" new hopefuls reach the Land of Israel during this period.

Millions of Jews are less lucky; they are desperate to get out of Germany and from all the other small nations that have recently been swallowed by the Nazi wolf. And even if they do manage to get out, where do they go?

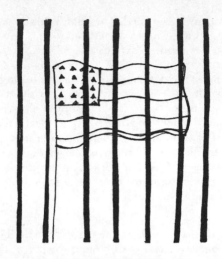

Restrictions on immigration are increasing in every country all over the world; even the Golden Door, the gate of America, is closing. The Jews of Europe are in despair, nobody wants to know. Many countries sympathize, but rationalize. Unfortunately there is nothing they can do, they would like to help, but they have their own problems. "Sorry." They shrug, they turn their backs. As always, a few do manage to escape the dragnet and reach South Africa, Central Africa and even Shanghai, but these are a mere trickle. The main bulk of European Jewry is trapped in the cage with the beast, who for the moment bides his time. America makes a gesture. The President, Franklin Delano Roosevelt, calls an international conference to discuss ways and means of saving European Jewry. It sounds impressive. The conference is held at Evian-les-Bains, in France. It is a dismal failure.

Desperation breeds desperate solutions.

Aliyah Bet is set up in response to the darkening climate. Jews are struggling to escape, but the world seems to shrug, to wash its hands of the problem. Aliyah Bet is a secret organisation set up in Palestine to try to do something about the plight of Jewish brethren trapped in Europe. The Aliyah Bet operation becomes a significant factor in bringing Jews to Palestine. 15,000 manage to enter the country by clandestine means during these last months of peace. Mossad is set up to organise and co-ordinate this "illegal" immigration. Meanwhile men and women of the Haganah are scouring abroad, secretly buying boats, decrepit, dilapidated old vessels that will somehow bring some remnants of Jewry to some sort of safety. And in Europe an "underground railroad" is being set up so that these Jews can actually reach these old boats. But...

120

The British are vigilant. The Arabs must be appeased and the British are pretty good in this area at the moment. And they are efficient. Only a few ships actually reach the shores of the Holy Land. Some flounder on the way and sink, their passengers drowning in the sea. Most boats are intercepted by the British. Two in particular, the Colorado and the Atrato, crammed with Polish Jews, are turned back and forced to return to Poland. Pragmatism rules Brittania. Thus, one of the blackest chapters in human history has opened. International dishonour becomes acceptable. You could say that such a terrible world deserves such a terrible destiny. The world doesn't have to wait very long.

Moscow August 23rd, 1939. Herr Joachim Von Ribbentrop, German Foreign Minister, arrives in the Russian capital. During the night he and Molotov, Russian Foreign Minister, do a deal. They sign a pact that guarantees "Neutrality and Non-Aggression" between their two countries. It is a bolt from the blue. The world is stunned, shocked, horrified. This an adroit move by Hitler; by achieving

Paul Celan

throughout the night. They will soon go out; the world has just a few days left before it turns into a lunatic asylum.

Poland. September 1st, 1939. 0445 hours. Hitler's army and airforce attack. "Operation White" begins. A merciless bombardment announces that the bloodiest tragedy in the history of the world has begun. The gates are closed on Nazi-occupied Europe. The Jews are sealed within the terrible fortress. Millions of Jews shake their heads. The British appeasers are silent; the mealy-mouthed, the weak-kneed, the Hitler-lovers finally get the message; even The Times gets the message. You cannot talk to Herr Hitler. Now it is time to dig deep shelters, put on the uniform, take up the gun. There is no other choice.

September 3rd, 1939. Britain and France have sent an ultimatum to Hitler; unless he stops attacking Poland and withdraws from that country a state of war will exist. The Nazis ignore the Allies and continue their reign and rain of terror. World War II begins and all hell breaks loose. It will be the worst nightmare that civilization has ever witnessed. Paul Celan, Jewish poet, will survive a concentration camp, but later will commit suicide. One of his greatest poems is called Fugue of Death. "Death is a master who comes from Germany." A chilling memorial for the burial of hope.

Russian neutrality the way is open for his total conquest of Europe. The great beast will slumber on the sidelines while he digests the rest of the world. That at least is the intention. Communists all over the world can hardly believe it; their deadly enemy has overnight become a sort of friend. They feel totally betrayed; it is almost unbelievable. It's as if Jesus Christ has suddenly joined the Devil.

Many will never recover from the act of cynical betrayal. Hitler rubs his hands with joy. First he will digest Poland. Russia can wait a little longer. Politicians scoot around the world, lights burn

Palestine. The Jews of the Yishuv realize that they have moved from centre stage. The World War overshadows all regional disputes. But the Jews of Palestine are still incensed with MacDonald's White Paper, even though they know they have no choice but to align themselves with Great Britain during the terrifying war ahead. Naturally this creates a schism, a duality in their attitude that is not easy to resolve. But Ben Gurion resolves the problem brilliantly. He sums it up succinctly in his famous rejoinder:

"We will fight the White Paper as if there were no war and fight the war as if there were no White Paper."

1940 April. Germany invades Norway and Denmark. Resistance is soon crushed. But of all people in Europe under the Nazi yoke the Danes will acquit themselves with extraordinary courage, managing to rescue most of their Jewish brethren from the Nazi death machine. The Danish Jews will prove to be a lucky and unique community.

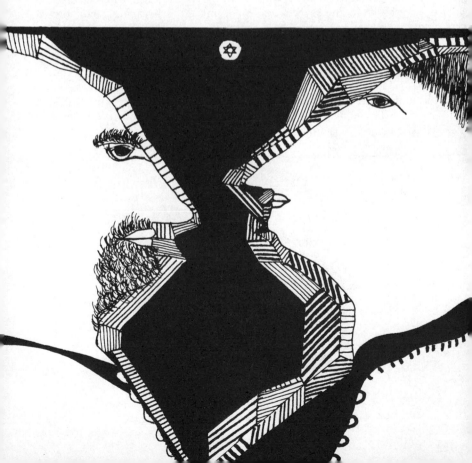

May. Germany launches a surprise attack upon Holland, Belgium and France. Resistance is quickly overcome. France crumbles; Frenchmen cry, unbelieving as Hitler's legions march into Paris. The corruption and cynicism of their leaders has largely contributed to this sudden collapse. But in Germany the people rejoice. The German nation basks in the success that their master is bringing them; the people believe that they have cancelled out the shame and the ignominy that the last war brought. Germany is now feared and respected. For the moment everything is coming up barking dogs and barbed wire. Tenders are invited from leading manufacturers. The German nation needs well-made incinerators, crematoria. It is the twilight of the world. When you start burning books and all the books are burned, you next look around for something else to burn. The Jews are the people of the book.

1940 Palestine. 136,000 Jewish volunteers register for national service with the British. They are determined to fight the common enemy; almost the entire Jewish population between the ages 18 and 50 wish to be involved.

November. Against all the odds refugee boats are still arriving from Europe. You would have thought that the British would by now had seen the light. You would be wrong. They have the temerity to intern those refugees who have actually reached the shores of the Holy Land. They decide to deport these Jews. The first deportation ship, the Patria, is about to sail for Mauritius with 1,700 people on board. It is sabotaged by the Haganah to prevent its departure, but things go tragically wrong. The boat sinks in Haifa Bay. 250 refugees are drowned. The British blink. Shortly after, they deport another group of 1,645 refugees to the island of Mauritius.

Frustrated by their failure to win air superiority against the British and thus invade and subjugate Great Britain, the Germans look eastward. In April 1941 they invade Yugoslavia and Greece. On June 22nd, 1941, Germany attacks Russia, launching an invasion along a 2,000 mile front. They advance relentlessly to the outskirts of Leningrad and Moscow.

December 7th, 1941. In the early morning the Japanese attack the main American naval base in Pearl Harbor in Hawaii. This cynical attack is devastating and takes place without a declaration of war. The American losses are considerable, but America is inexhaustible. They are now in the war with Britain and Russia, against Germany and Japan. They recover from the initial attack. Their supplies and men will pour in from now onward; this will prove a major turning point in this desperate war. "The Yanks are coming." That old song from the pen of that most Jewish American of American Jews, Irving Berlin, resounds around the world, gives a modicum of hope in this twilight of the world.

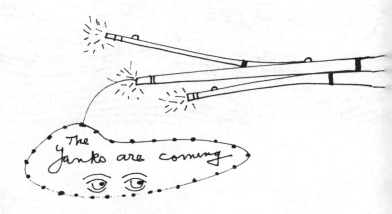

1941 December. Chelmno. The first extermination camp set up by the Nazis comes into operation. The first mass murder of Jews takes place.

1942 January 20, Wannsee, Germany: At this conference the official German plans for "the Final Solution" are secretly set out. Details for mass murder are specified; the number of Jews in each country is worked out, methods for their deportation and extermination arranged. German statisticians are working overtime. Their wives are pleased because it brings in some extra money; but they are working through the night—nobody appreciates how hard it is to murder the world's 18 million Jews. It is a really big problem.

February. The Struma is carrying refugees from Roumania. But the British, God bless 'em and all who sail in them, can have none of that. These Jews must not be allowed to land in Palestine. This is a remarkable decision at a time when most Arabs are siding with the

Nazis and most Palestinian Jews are desperate to fight with the Allies. But the ways of the British government are even more mysterious than the ways of God. The Turkish government heeds the British request and the Struma is turned back. It flounders in the Black Sea. 770 refugees lose their lives.

Jewish volunteers are now being accepted for service by the British in the Middle East, which has become a huge military base. Gradually these volunteers are welded into Jewish units with Jewish officers in command. They render invaluable service in Libya, Egypt, Ethiopia, Greece and Crete. By the end of 1942 these Jewish companies have become three Jewish infantry battalions. The British attitude towards Haganah has changed; now they are expected to help the war effort. The Palmach ("striking force") has already been established and is a regular full-time force. As the German threat to the Middle East grows, the British call in Haganah to help them in the invasion of Syria; hundreds of Palmach soldiers are trained by the British in commando and sabotage techniques. One way or another, more than 20,000 Palestinian Jews will fight with the Allies before the end of this war.

By the end of 1942 the Yishuv in Palestine is becoming aware of the appalling fate of their brethren in the death camps. Plans are made to try and rescue some of the victims, but the British will not hear of it. They regard these efforts as a violation of the White Paper. The White Paper seems to be a wonderful excuse for lethargy and indifference.

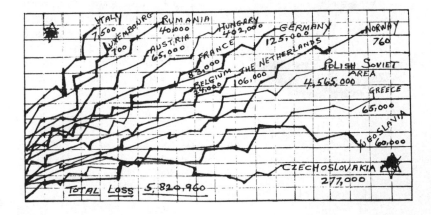

Eventually several thousand Jews manage to straggle to Istanbul and, notwithstanding the obstruction of the British, they do finally reach Palestine. Another project, to drop Haganah parachutists into occupied Europe and rouse Jewish youth to resist the Nazis, is also severely obstructed by the British. It amounts to nothing.

Stalingrad, Russia. September 1942. The furthest point the Germans penetrate into Russia. But the German army is resisted street by street by the Russians. Eventually the besiegers are besieged; the Russians win a famous victory. The victorious German army now tastes bitter defeat. Twenty-one German divisions have fought here—and lost. The Russians take 90,000 prisoners. Now the course of the war seems to turn; a kind of psychological Rubicon is crossed.

1943 America. US State Department rejects Swedish proposal to rescue 20,000 Jewish children from Germany.

Warsaw. The ghetto of Warsaw is cramped. It is surrounded by newly-built walls, barbed wire and Nazi guards. 450,000 Jews live within these walls. It is April 19th, 1943: Passover, the first Seder night. The Nazis are ready to move in, to clear the entire population, to remove them to the death camps. But the Jews have other ideas.

Much to the astonishment of the Nazi SS General Stroop these Jews actually resist. Every man, woman and child of the ghetto becomes a fighter. It is a life and death battle. House to house, street to street, through sewers and underground tunnels. The battle rages. For four weeks the Jews resist. It is a heroic, but hopeless task; a story of human hands tearing at the armed might of Germany. Most of the Jews are killed in the battle, but the story of their resistance spreads all over the world. The ghetto is finally consumed in fire and blood.

May 16th, 1943. After four weeks of continuous fighting General Stroop sends a message to his superiors in Berlin. "The former Jewish

residential district (German euphemism for ghetto) in Warsaw no longer exists." One song perhaps typifies the spirit of those Jewish fighters who battled against impossible odds. This song, Zog Nit Keynmol (Oh Never Say), is written by Hirsh Glik, gifted young poet of Vilna who escapes twice from concentration camps, fights with the partisans, is killed in battle.

"Oh never say that we have reached the end

... the hour we yearn for will still come

... from a land of palm trees to a snow-laden land we travel on

... this song was written in blood, not pencil.

It is not the happy song of birds,

but of people who, with walls crashing about them,

sang it with grenades in their hands!''

The Jews of Warsaw are wiped out, fighting. Their action is their epitaph.

May 7th,1945. Rheims, France. Hitler is already dead. On this day in this ancient French city the Germans accept unconditional surrender. The war in Europe is over.

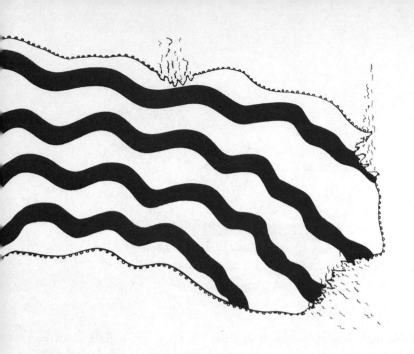

But only now does the full truth emerge. Six million Jews have been murdered in the death camps. Six million! Numbers numb; the brain finds it hard to absorb such information. One third of the entire Jewish world population! And all this happened while the rest of the world blinked. A whole culture has been destroyed. How do you tune in to six million individual lives. How can you feel the loss, the hollow? It defies logic, reason. Words have lost their meaning. Only the silence of those six million can speak for them. All we have are words to try to understand, to speak for them. And in the end all we have are two words to try to say it all.

And around those words — the suffering, the silence.

Two words:

The silence.

Two words:

Six million.

Two words:

The holocaust.

No attempt at understanding the catastrophe proves adequate. The world emerges from war in a state of shock. The Germans shake their heads in seeming disbelief. They did not know. How could they know? Could they have behaved in such a manner had they known? It defies logic, reason. Humans simply do not behave like this. Hitler's favourite operatic piece is the Twilight of the Gods, by none other than Gotterdämmerung Wagner. In this even the gods are destroyed as the whole underworld goes up in fire and smoke. It appears that Hitler wants this for Germany. If they cannot win the war then they must all be consumed by flames. When victory finally appears to be impossible he demands this catharsis for the German people. Possibly he wanted to play out this death wish from the very beginning. He is Anti-man. Anti-human. Anti-life. The Jews are merely a rehearsal for the main event. To call him a madman, a monster is an easy way out; it absolves from the need to understand how one human can order other humans to behave in such an inhuman manner towards other humans. We have to understand why they carried out the orders. Hitler cannot, must not, be pigeonholed and explained away. For he may well be the terrible future, the dehumanizing agent who can take out an entire city without flinching, a whole people, a whole civilization without a shrug.

But one German tries to understand.

Niemoeller A German Christian pastor bravely defies the Nazis, writes about the modern Dark Ages, when the Black Death is rampant in Germany. This is how he sums it up.

"First they came for the Jews
and I did not speak out— because I was not a Jew.
Then they came for the communists
and I did not speak out—because I was not a communist
Then they came for the trade unionists and I did not
speak out— because I was not a trade unionist.
Then they came for me—
and there was no one left to speak out for me."

(There are others like him. And, at Yad Vashem, the Holocaust Museum in Jerusalem, there is an "Avenue of the Righteous" for the few who cared and helped the very few; people like Raoul Wallenberg, who saved thousands in Budapest.)

All people who on earth do dwell . . . can rejoice. But those under the earth, those who have slipped away in smoke, cannot rejoice. Neither can those Jewish remnants who survived them. When the enormity of the crime is revealed, it stuns the world.

The world, though, is also caught up in the rejoicing that the war has ended. But there is little rejoicing amongst the Jews of the world. Thoughts and eyes turn to the survivors, to bring them out of the disease-ridden and ravaged camps. Thoughts naturally turn to Palestine.

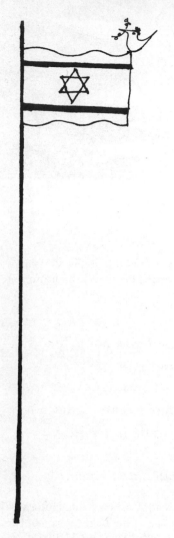

The unutterable facts of the war become the seed-corn for a new determination that this can never happen again. Under any circumstances, no matter what the costs, the statehood of the Jewish people now needs to be a reality. This new element of despair is added to all the other elements and urgency that is in the air. **There must be independence.**

August 1945. President Truman appeals to the British Prime Minister, Clement Attlee, to permit the immigration of 100,000 Jews into Palestine. These displaced persons, these refugees, are languishing in desperation—the problem is acute. Where can they go? Attlee is the leader of the British Labour Party. They have recently won an overwhelming victory in the General Election and now have power. The British Labour Party has always been sympathetic to the Zionist cause and there is hope that there will now be a favourable change in British policy towards the Yishuv. But these hopes are soon dashed. Some people say that Ernest Bevin, the Foreign Secretary, is a virulent anti-semite. Others believe they are closer to the truth and drop the word "virulent". The Palmach, the Irgun Zva Le'umi and Lehi continue their attacks upon British installations. There are frequent clashes between security forces and Jewish demonstrators in Palestine. The atmosphere is highly charged and this tension prevails throughout. An Anglo-American commission arrives after visiting Displaced Persons Camps in Europe. Its report, submitted on May 1st, recommends the immediate admission of 100,000 Jewish refugees. The British government rejects this recommendation.

June 17th,1946. The Jewish underground responds to the British by blowing up the bridges linking Palestine with neighbouring states.

June 29th. The British government responds to these attacks by arresting the members of the Jewish Agency Executive. This day is known as "Black Sabbath". The British response is thorough. They confiscate secret documents, send military forces to search dozens of settlements. They make exhaustive searches for arms and discover an enormous arms cache at Kibbutz Yagur. These searches continue for several days. Thousands of suspected members of the "illegal" army are rounded up and interned in camps at Rafa. More refugee boats are stopped in the Mediterranean. More Jews are interned in Cyprus. Tension is at fever pitch.

July 22nd. The British Central Government offices are sited at the King David Hotel in Jerusalem. The Irgun Zva Le'umi blow it up. Eighty people are killed. Government officials and civilians, Britons, Jews and Arabs are amongst the victims. The seed-corn of desperation is sprouting. Pandora's box is opened. It is hard to underestimate the bitterness felt at this time all round the world. The Jews in Britain smart under the blows of British public opinion incensed at the outrage. This inevitable reaction causes a deep dichotomy amongst Jews in the Diaspora. Some want a quiet life. Some are strident in their defence of this extreme Jewish action in Palestine. Nothing has changed, it appears. Jews were never destined to lead a quiet life.

The Jewish Agency in Palestine orders a halt to the armed actions against the British, but the Revisionist movement refuses to listen. The British government is trying to break up Haganah and the many

diverse elements that form this army. The British government aim to bring about the formation of a more moderate Jewish leadership. but soon realizes that this objective cannot be achieved.

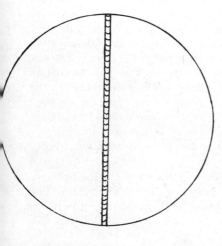

After a few weeks, the interned Jewish leaders are set free.

The British open negotiations with Jewish and Arab leaders in 1947. The British submit a new proposal which provides for the division of Palestine into three sectors—Jewish, Arab and British. The British section is to include Jerusalem and the Negev and the British are to retain supreme control for another four years. Jews and Arabs reject this proposal. The British Government announces in February that it wants to wash its hands of the

whole affair and is handing over the Palestine problem to the United Nations, lock, stock and barrel. But their attitude remains as intransigent as ever with regard to further immigration into Palestine during this interim period.

Terror continues.

The Irgun and Lehi are attacking military and government installations. They make a most spectacular attack upon the fortress prison of Acre, and free several of their comrades. The British government respond with further stern measures. The British capture several Revisionist soldiers. The British call them "terrorists". The Irgun call them "freedom fighters". The British hang seven of their captives. The Irgun retaliate by hanging two British sergeants that they have captured. Desperate days. In Great Britain windows of synagogues are broken.

May. The Palestinian problem comes before a special session of the United Nations General Assembly.

To everyone's surprise Andrei Gromyko, the Soviet delegate, expresses his government's support for the right of Jews to establish their own state in Palestine. The United Nations recommends the partition of Palestine into two separate states, Jewish and Arab, and this state to be joined by an economic union.

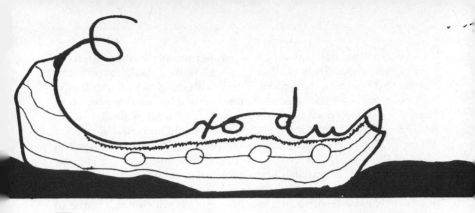

The **Exodus 1947** arrives in Haifa in July with 4,500 refugees aboard. The British refuse to allow the refugees to land; the boat is forced to return to its French port of departure. But the refugees refuse to disembark there. The British take the boat to Hamburg in their Occupation Zone where the passengers are forcibly taken off and dumped on the soil of dreaded Germany. The British have not been very clever. They have been at diplomacy a long time. One would have thought that they might have a little more sensitivity. This action does more for the Jewish cause than anything else. It focuses world opinion. The British receive the opprobrium of the world. The Jews of Palestine are stirred to rebellion. Acts of sabotage proliferate. The British are now reinforced in their view that they must give up the Mandate. The moment of truth seems to be arriving.

November 29th. The General Assembly of the United Nations accepts the majority recommendation. There is to be a Jewish state that is to consist of Eastern Galilee, the northern part of the Jordan Valley, the Beth Shean and Jezreel Valleys, the coastal strip from south of Acre to south of Rehovot, and the Negev desert including Eilat. Jerusalem is to have international status. The other parts of the country, just about 50%, are to form an Arab state. The British government announces that it will not co-operate in the execution of this plan and will withdraw its entire administration and military forces on May 15th, 1948. The Yishuv receives the news with jubilation. The Arab states denounce the United Nations decision and state that they are determined to solve the problem by force.

November 30th sees Arab violence. Mobs run riot. Buses are fired on, Jews killed. The Arabs call a general strike. Arabs attack the commercial quarter of Jerusalem. The British stand by and watch idly. The Haganah is unprepared and the commercial quarter goes up in flames. Riots spread all over the country. The scale is similar to the riots of 1936 and 1939 during the Arab revolt, but now there is a difference; the Jews are alone facing the Arab bands. The British watch while chaos is king. The defence of the Yishuv now becomes the sole responsibility of Haganah. There are great problems maintaining contact with isolated Jewish villages. Jerusalem is besieged by Arab bands and heavy Jewish casualties are sustained during this battle to maintain communications. Convoys on the road to Ben Shemen, the Etzion Bloc and Jerusalem are destroyed. There is a strict rationing of food and water. Jewish premises are blown up. There is a desperate lack of arms. The struggle is bitter and widespread.

April 1948. Large consignments of arms arrive from Czechoslovakia. It brings an immediate improvement to the situation of the Jews of the Yishuv. Israel is about to be born in blood and fire but the world has grave doubts. It is standing around watching this birth, shaking its head. Surely the baby will be stillborn. **It cannot possibly survive.**

There is a dramatic change in the course of the fighting. Haganah seize the initiative, establish a hold on all the territories that have been alloted to the Jewish state. The road to Jerusalem is cleared. Large convoys of food are rushed to the beleaguered city.

The Revisionist Irgun Zva Le'umi and Lehi forces attack the village of Deir Yasin west of Jerusalem in April. Many innocent Arab civilians are killed, some say murdered. The Arabs accuse the Revisionists of

this massacre; the Revisionists deny responsibility, saying that the killings were necessary under the circumstances, an act of self-defence. The controversy over this episode continues to this day.

Jews need to believe that fellow Jews could never resort to such inhuman acts. Many Jews throughout the world believe that the Jews must be a light unto the nations, that they must be a more moral people than anyone else, that they have an obligation to humanity because of the way they have suffered.

Arabs are panicking but their forces launch a major attack upon Mishmar Ha-Emek aiming to break through to Haifa. They are completely routed. Safad is liberated, but Arab terrorists ambush a convoy of Jewish doctors, nurses and teachers on their way to the Hadassah hospital on Mount Scopus. Seventy-seven persons killed.

On April 18th, Tiberias is taken by Jewish forces.

April 22nd. Haganah battle for and occupy the whole of Haifa. Hundreds of thousands of Arabs flee from the area occupied by Jewish forces. The Jewish leadership will insist that this mass flight is encouraged by the Arab leadership, who spread rumours of atrocities that will be dealt upon the Arab population as soon as the Jewish forces take control. The Arab leaders also ask their brothers to clear the way for the advancing Arab armies. The Arabs deny it: the controversy continues until this day.

It is the eve of the British departure from their association with the Holy Land. Haganah seize most of new Jerusalem. The Jewish quarter in the Old City is besieged and cut off by forces of the Arab Legion, a Jordanian unit commanded by British officers. The Arab Legion overruns the Jewish forces on May 13th. On this same day, Jaffa surrenders to Haganah.

By the middle of May, the Jews have suffered 2,500 fatal casualties.

May 14th. The British at last give up their Mandate and leave Palestine. It is a long association. They seem to be glad to get rid of it. The Jews at once set up a provisional government. The State of Israel is proclaimed. David Ben Gurion is the first Prime Minister.

It has been an unbelievably long
journey from Abraham to this
present day. The umbiblical cord
twisting and turning through
history has at last brought forth its
fruit.

Israel Is.

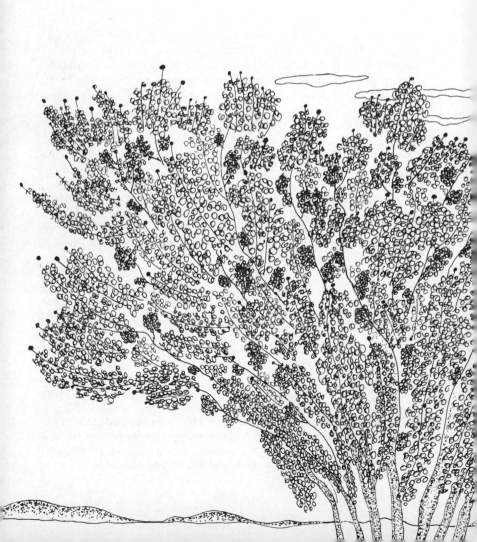

The State of Israel is proclaimed. All over the world Jews rejoice. They have their own independent state. At long last there is a point of focus, a counterpoint to the diaspora. This will change their fate, bring them a new pride, afford them a new respect. Jews the world over will now enjoy a new peace of mind by owning their own piece of land.

They have their own elected parliament, their own government, their own opposition; their own schools, hospitals, street sweepers. They can be allowed the luxury of making their own mistakes; they can take their place among all the other nations of the world. Israel exists in reality.

But this new state is not greeted with universal acclaim. The Arabs are not so happy; they feel that Israel is a threat to their way of life. They decide to wipe the new nation off the map, off the earth. The Arabs choose a symbol, epitomising their intention—the Star of David with a knife slashing into it. The attack follows the intention. Israel is immediately assailed from all sides. The fighting is bitter and land is lost. The Arabs push and push, threatening Tel Aviv and Jerusalem. The Jews are poorly armed but they fight back with bitter intent. The knowledge of the recent holocaust is still seared into their souls and they are possessed with burning zeal; they know that they simply cannot be defeated. Against all the odds they regain much land, and not only the land originally granted by the United Nations, but more. They push the Arabs further and further back. Israel soon consolidates and flourishes, an island of creative ambition surrounded by seething hatred.

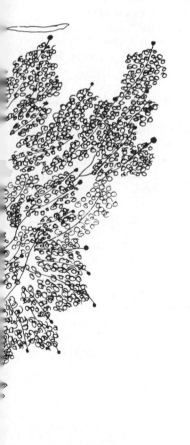

Jews have always asked questions and the children of the new Israel are no exception to the Hebrew ethos. The State of Israel poses more questions than it answers.

Thousands of Arabs have left Israel during the fighting. Did they jump or were they pushed? Whatever the truth, how can the world deal with this enormous human problem, the refugee camps filled with the homeless and the hopeless throughout the Arab world? And what about the refugee problem on the other side? The hundreds of thousands of Jews fleeing Arab countries for Israel, stripped of their citizenship? These refugees are welcome in the new state, but the resources of Israel are stretched to the limit. And beyond.

But independence releases a new energy: a million immigrants are absorbed in the space of a few years; immigrant transit camps are converted into new towns; dozens of kibbutzim are set up; synagogues and hospitals are established all over the country. Jews all over the world rally to Israel's support. They come as volunteers, they send money; they identify with the new state even if most of them do not want to settle there; it is as meaningful to them as the health of their family. If Israel is threatened they themselves feel threatened. This partnership is for better or worse; it is on a deep emotional level, it cannot be severed.

In Israel life continues and becomes more complex. The Jews always wanted to be like all the other nations. Now their dream is realized. With a vengeance. They are like other nations, only more so. Political parties proliferate. Jews argue. They argue about politics, they argue about arguing. Extremists of the right and the left argue among themselves, producing even more extreme extremists, while even moderates of the centre create multifarious variations.

There seems to be no end to crisis. So what's new? For the Jews life has always been a crisis. Get rid of this crisis and who knows? . . . an even greater crisis could take its place. Thought for the day. Learn to love your crisis. This certainly seems to be the way of things in the new Israel.

But life goes on. Agriculture booms, industry expands, science flourishes. The young argue with their parents. Writers and poets, artists and actors, all express what it means to be an Israeli, all in their own specific way. Israel is a patchwork of ideas and people, arguing yet living in a kind of vibrant, audacious harmony.

And underneath it all there is the same urgent need to ask questions. The children of Jacob are still struggling with the angel, are still questioning the meaning of their existence. In Israel this urgency never recedes because the threat of extinction is always there. This living on a knife edge doesn't make for a quiet life.

Where are we going?

What kind of life do we want for ourselves and our children?

Have we lost our way?

Can we go on continuously fighting war after war?

Can we go on being bled of our most valuable resources, our children?

Are we doing the right thing?

What does it all mean?

Despite the obvious problems, despite all the questions that remain unanswered, unresolved, despite the endless crises, despite the seemingly impossible situation—the dream persists. The dream simply will not lie down. This dream is in their bones, in the will of the Jewish people, the will, not only to survive but to succeed. This will appears to be unquenchable. This determination comes with mother's milk. The Jewish people have no other choice but to look to the future.

It has taken more than three decades for even one Arab state, Egypt, to take the initiative and have the courage to break ranks with their Arab brothers and sign a peace treaty with the State of Israel. How long can this present state of no peace - no war continue? Every decade since the State of Israel was proclaimed has produced at least one bloody war. 1948. 1956. 1967. 1973. 1982. The bloody litany of death and horror seems without end. Young boys die on both sides. Children shudder under bombardment, parents weep; young brides wear black. The Arabs claim the land is theirs and want it back. The Jews say one holocaust was one too many. Israel sticks in the gullet of the Arab people; it is an anathema to them. The Israelis say... if you recognise us we can talk about everything... unless you recognise us we can talk about nothing. Churchill said, "Jaw, jaw is better than war, war."

The Israelis refuse to retreat from the land so dearly won. A land they never lost sight of . . . through all the thousands of years of exile; a land they believe is their very own—a land they never really relinquished . . . Their obsession with archaeology is an obsession with the need to rediscover the roots of their own long past. The Israelis would die on their own land rather than give it up. The Arabs believe that this land was taken from them and want it back. They believe that strangers are occupying their land and swear they will take it back, by blood and fire if necessary. Both sides have claims. It is a case of two claims producing one enormous tragedy—war and suffering. But if both sides are not to share a common graveyard, then an accommodation must be reached sooner or later. **Compromise is not a dirty word.** The only alternative to war is compromise . . . and for Israel and the Arabs also read the future of the world. In this small part of the Middle East . . . the destiny of the Jews happens to be the usual litmus test for the future of humanity.

All over the world, ever since man crawled out of the mud, he knows that somehow he must survive, and for this he has to resolve seemingly impossible situations. He must compromise. People will simply have to sit down and talk. Jew and Arab. Well before Israel came into being, Albert Einstein said:

"Peace cannot be kept by force, it can only be achieved by understanding."